CAPTURING MARIPOSAS

COGNITIVE APPROACHES TO CULTURE

Frederick Luis Aldama, Patrick Colm Hogan,
Lalita Pandit Hogan, and Sue J. Kim, Series Editors

CAPTURING MARIPOSAS

READING CULTURAL SCHEMA IN GAY CHICANO LITERATURE

DOUG P. BUSH

THE OHIO STATE UNIVERSITY PRESS
COLUMBUS

Copyright © 2019 by The Ohio State University.
All rights reserved.

Library of Congress Cataloging-in-Publication Data
Names: Bush, Doug P., author.
Title: Capturing mariposas : reading cultural schema in gay Chicano literature / Doug P. Bush.
Other titles: Cognitive approaches to culture.
Description: Columbus : The Ohio State University Press, [2019] | Series: Cognitive approaches to culture | Includes bibliographical references and index.
Identifiers: LCCN 2018041540| ISBN 9780814213889 (cloth ; alk. paper) | ISBN 081421388X (cloth ; alk. paper)
Subjects: LCSH: American literature—Mexican American authors—History and criticism. | Gay men's writings, American—History and criticism. | Mexican American gays—Intellectual life.
Classification: LCC PS153.G38 B87 2019 | DDC 810.9/92066408968—dc23
LC record available at https://lccn.loc.gov/2018041540

Cover design by Laurence J. Nozik
Text design by Juliet Williams
Type set in Adobe Minion Pro

♾ The paper used in this publication meets the minimum requirements of the American National Standard for Information Sciences—Permanence of Paper for Printed Library Materials. ANSI Z39.48-1992.

CONTENTS

Acknowledgments   vii

INTRODUCTION   Genre, Schema, and Looking Beyond the Artifact   1

CHAPTER 1   Can You Feel Me? Affect and Cross-Understanding in *Crossing Vines* and *Butterfly Boy*   21

CHAPTER 2   Sexual Shame: Bridging Muñoz's Vague Narrator   57

CHAPTER 3   Unexpected Surprises and the Magic Realization of Espinoza's *Still Water Saints*   85

CHAPTER 4   Market and Reader   115

CHAPTER 5   Conversations with the Authors   143

CONCLUSION   Branching Out   159

Works Cited   165

Index   177

ACKNOWLEDGMENTS

THIS BOOK would not have been possible without the guidance and support of Frederick Luis Aldama, who pushed me at every step of the way. I have no idea how Frederick finds the time to do everything that he does, but I am eternally grateful that he pulled me into his orbit back in 2011. This has included being a recipient of the inaugural LASER/Humanities Institute Fellowship at The Ohio State University and providing countless opportunities to meet both authors and other scholars in the field.

I also extend gratitude to both Ignacio Corona at Ohio State and Juan Armando Rojas Joo at Ohio Wesleyan University, both of whom have served as exemplary advisors and mentors. Along with Frederick, I could not have asked for a better trio to lead me into the academic world. And to Converse College for plucking me off the job market when I was ready to give up altogether and providing generous support for the publication of this book.

Thanks to the Andrew W. Mellon Foundation for their Ohio 5 Colleges Postdoctoral Fellowship program. The two-year support that this program provided in residence at Ohio Wesleyan University was fundamental in the realization of this project.

I have received invaluable insights from countless numbers of readers, and here would like to thank in particular Sue J. Kim and Patrick Colm Hogan, who helped to reshape the introduction, as well the anonymous reader who completely brutalized a previous draft, leading to fundamental changes that greatly strengthened the final project. I have no idea who you are and hope to never find out, but thank you for the very constructive criticism. I also extend thanks to the members of the Association for Jotería Arts, Activism and Scholarship, who have given me so much to think about with their invaluable essays and other works, the footprints of which are evident in much of this book.

I owe a deep debt to Kristen Elias Rowley, editor in chief at OSU Press, as well as their editorial board and entire crew for seeing the value in this project and being so supportive along the way. I would also like to extend a special thanks to both Manuel Muñoz and Alex Espinoza for being so generous with their time during our extensive interviews.

On a personal note, a warm hug to colleagues and friends who were always present with emotional support throughout this long process, including Amanda, Chantal, Indra, Mariana, Theresa, and so many others. Thank you for keeping me physically active and socially present when it would have been so much easier to be neither.

To Marco, my partner in life, thank you for uprooting your sunny California life and moving to Ohio so that I could pursue a PhD. Thank you too for being patient, covering the bills, offering endless support, and continually pushing me to just "get it done." And yes, you can retire now.

And finally, thanks to my grandmother Eva, who raised me as her own, and always beamed with pride with every step I took up the academic ladder, even if she wasn't quite sure what it all meant. Even though I lost you in May 2018, without you none of this would have been possible.

INTRODUCTION

Genre, Schema, and Looking Beyond the Artifact

IN THE 2014 COLLECTION *Queer in Aztlán*, Pablo Alvarez recounts the teenage joy of discovering the gay and lesbian section at his local bookstore and how he visited in eager anticipation once a month hoping to finally encounter a Chicanx name somewhere on the shelf. Although he admits that this strategy did result in overlooking John Rechy, it did eventually bring him to Gil Cuadros's 1994 collection *City of God,* published just two years before his death. Alvarez recalls "slid[ing] the book out of the stack . . . and feel[ing] a familiarity with the front cover of the book design" (294)—an upside-down image of Los Angeles and rows of prayer candles staring back at him. He writes that "I drove home that night captivated by the pages I read while waiting at red lights" (294) because Cuadros's work "reflected a reality that I understood" (294). His recollection is heavily marked by the identificatory power of that experience—as he recounts, "every range of emotion was triggered with each turning of a page" because Cuadros's words "spoke to my own desires and fears" (294).

Alvarez's recollection of finding and devouring *City of God* is a powerful example of two of the main themes of this book: the importance of genre and the power of reader identification with literature.

While Alvarez encountered challenges in finding gay Chicanx voices in the 1990s, it likely would not be as difficult today—production of gay Chicano literature has exploded in recent years, with authors such as Alex Espinoza, Rigoberto González, Manuel Muñoz, Benjamin Alire Sáenz, and Alex Sánchez publishing dozens of texts since the turn of the millennium. Their production comes on the heels of those who established their careers in the decades prior—including John Rechy, Francisco X. Alarcón, Arturo Islas, Richard Rodriguez, and Michael Nava[1]—who, combined, have expanded into just about every type of output imaginable: novels, poetry, biographies, young adult and children's fiction, and expository works.[2] Tallying up their collective output, we can chart the emergence of a unique literary genre, or at the very least a distinct subgenre, just as the more widely recognized Chicana feminists emerged into their own more than thirty years ago. Just as those women did, the authors of this genre are actively creating community both for and with their readers, providing an identificatory space that may not have otherwise existed. As Alvarez's example demonstrates, the creation of this space is particularly important for those youngest readers, and indeed, a good part of Rigoberto González's 2013 work, *Red-Inked Retablos,* is dedicated to that generation of readers, culminating in

---

1. While there is a case to be made for dividing these authors into generations, their production has also overlapped considerably. Although Islas's literary career was cut short by his death from complications of HIV/AIDS, Rechy's career has spanned more than fifty years since publishing his landmark *City of Night* in 1963, and Alarcón published frequently in the 1980s through the 2000s. While the majority of Nava's work was confined to the 1980s and 1990s, he has become active once again, after a thirteen-year break, with the release of *City of Palaces* in 2014 and *Lay Your Sleeping Head* in late 2016. I group Espinoza, González, Muñoz, Sáenz, and Sánchez because the vast majority of their work has come since the turn of the millennium and they are, as of the writing of this book, still active in producing new works.

2. This list excludes gay Chicano voices found outside of the literary canon, which Richard T. Rodríguez looks at in his essay "Carnal Knowledge." For Rodríguez, a thorough recuperation of gay Chicano subjectivity in literature must include archival research, which he performs in sources as disparate as Joe Olvera's poem "Gay Ghetto District," published in 1980 in *Flor y Canto IV & V*; a 1981 interview with a gay Chicano appearing in the lowrider magazine *Firme*; and the 1985 gay Chicano poetry collection *Ya vas, carnal,* which features Alarcón.

the powerful yet humorous mariposa[3] prayer (138–40), while *Queer in Aztlán* is filled with personal stories including coming out, finding community, and living with HIV/AIDS.[4]

---

3. I go on the assumption that most reading this book will be familiar with terms such as *mariposa*, a derogatory Spanish word for homosexual meaning "butterfly" that has been reclaimed by those whom it was meant to insult—see Pérez ("Toward") for a lineage of the word. I use a number of like terms in this book, taking cues from scholars in the field.

As of this writing, *jotería studies* seems to be the term of choice to describe the queer Chicanx/Latinx experience, with *jotería* being derived from the Mexican slang joto, meaning "fag/queer." This is reminiscent of Gloria Anzaldúa calling herself *dyke* because she did not feel that *queer* or *lesbian* adequately described who she was ("To(o) Queer" 264), or Jaime Manrique using *maricón* in reference to himself, Federico García Lorca, Manuel Puig, and Reinaldo Arenas, because they "had the *cojones* that many heterosexual writers lacked" (113). Nevertheless, as Bañalez explains, *jotería* also contains a more racial aspect: "Unlike the reclaiming of fag or other terms like dyke and queer the resignification of Jotería (and Joto/a) is a part of the decolonizing collective movement" (156). We must be mindful, however, that *jotería* may not be inclusive of the wider Latinx experience given that it is Mexican slang. Others, meanwhile, prefer *queer*; Del Castillo and Güido write in *Queer in Aztlán* that they prefer the term "for its inclination toward the uncommon, open, political and unpredictable possibilities" (xix). Nevertheless, *queer* does have its problems—in *Gay Latino Studies,* Hames-García and Martínez note that it tends to have "an investment in whiteness . . . and a Eurocentric insistence on whiteness as an unquestioned norm" (11). In our interview, Manuel Muñoz said much of the same—that he does not like the word *queer* because of its strong association with whiteness. In this book, I decided to follow the example set by Hames-García and Martínez in *Gay Latino Studies* where they outline a number of reasons for using the term *gay*, including the most simple: truth in advertising (10). Their collected essays are exclusively focused on *gay male* lives, just as this book focuses on *gay male* authors. This discussion does illuminate the importance of self-identification: Whether it be *joto, maricón, queer, dyke, fag, trans, bi,* or simply *gay*—terms that may be cringeworthy for some but worn as a badge of honor for others—how one chooses to identify themselves should be followed and respected.

4. Of course, any reader may read any book for whatever reason, but here I am more speaking to the idea and importance of role models, particularly those who reflect a reader's own ethnicity and sexuality. This is one of the great strengths of the Chicana feminist movement, forged by advocates such as Gloria Anzaldúa, Cherríe Moraga, Ana Castillo, Norma Alarcón, and Marta Cotera (to name just a few) who did not see their subjectivities reflected in the Chicanx and broader feminist movements, or saw both as overtly and

GENRE MATTER(S)

This discussion of genre is one of the most critical questions that I have faced. Does production by gay Chicano authors really need its own distinct label and space in the market? Why does it matter? After speaking with, teaching, and studying these authors and reading recollections such as those from Alvarez, I believe that these distinctions do matter because genre means both visibility and a constructive thread to place works within context of each other. Consider the opening example of what genre means to the ordinary reader. Academics have been working to put these authors in context with each other and exploring gay Chicano identities going back to the 1980s and 1990s with landmark (and often cited) articles and books from Almaguer, Bruce-Novoa, and Foster. However, had genre-building (and reader-directed) tomes such as *Red-Inked Retablos* and *Queer in Aztlán* existed then, Alvarez's search for that queer Chicano voice that spoke to him likely would not have been as lengthy. Aside from their mediations on queer Chicanx lives, *Retablos* mentions a slew of authors who may also interest the reader, while *Queer* caps itself with an extensive bibliography of both literary and academic sources.[5]

---

covertly antagonistic to their subjectivities (Moraga and Anzaldúa 61; Torres 156; Cotera 215; Pesquera and Segura 300). Given that the Chicana feminist movement has solidly established itself over the past few decades, there has been a drive to become more inclusive of Latinx males, particularly those who identify as queer (Anzaldúa, *Borderlands* 106–7; Moraga, *Xicana* 123), organizing under the more inclusive term *Xicano*, or more recent configurations such as *jotería studies*. Although Moraga has been somewhat antagonistic toward the early generation of gay Chicano authors—particularly Arturo Islas and Richard Rodriguez, whom she takes to task in "Queer Aztlán" for remaining in the closet (266–67)—she has also been welcoming to the younger generation, telling Weatherston that "every place that I have ever taught, young gay men of color have come to me and said, 'If it hadn't been for black lesbians, if it hadn't been for Chicana lesbians, I wouldn't know how to understand being queer.' ... Lesbians of color are making space for these young men" (70). What I suggest here is that gay authors themselves are now capable of providing this space and, moreover, are doing it, with their literary production and engagement with audiences as critical to this process.

5. Extensive, but not perfect—it does contain a few oversights, such as the exclusion of Manuel Muñoz, Alex Sánchez, and Benjamin Alire Sáenz.

The organizing impulse of genre is also critical in the academic setting, where we actively teach in these categories—consider groupings of writers that have become central to syllabi formation such as Asians, African Americans, queers, or Chicana feminist authors, to name but a few. Even with the increasing breadth of their production, gay Chicano authors have generally not carved out their own space in the classroom as a unique entity—that is, taught independently of larger groupings of Latinx and/or queer authors. For some readers, the classroom is where they will encounter this literature for the very first time, and it may be critical in the formation of their own sense of self.

Nevertheless, dedicated scholars in the field are working to rectify this lack of academic representation. While we can look to the work of Bruce-Novoa and Foster (among many) as being fundamental in the building up of this genre, its more recent configuration under the banner of jotería studies has served to strengthen its position even further. Jotería scholarship, that which focuses on the queer Chicanx/Latinx experience, is represented in important collections such as *Queer in Aztlán*; a lengthy dossier in the journal *Aztlán*, published in 2014; the collective AJAAS (Association of Jotería Arts, Activism, and Scholarship); and a number of other works that I will discuss later. As Hames-García writes in the introduction to the *Aztlán* dossier, jotería scholarship represents the making of space for "multigendered queer Chican@s and Latin@s, trained and nurtured by women of color feminisms and feminists," keeping in mind the "limitations of identity categories" (138). Rather than the author distancing themselves from the subject as is typical in academic writing, jotería studies exalts the personal experience, making it a base for theory (Hames-García 135; Revilla and Santillana 172). The *Aztlán* dossier includes important work on jotería pedagogy, the visual arts, and aesthetics, among others. This approach—transforming personal experience into theory—is also one of the underpinnings of *Queer in Aztlán,* which intends to be open to a general audience and encourage further scholarship and inclusion in course curricula (Del Castillo and Güido x). Another landmark is the 2011 collection *Gay Latino Studies,* which takes on the mission of "re-member"ing gay Latino studies by "bring[ing] together a coalitional body" of what has been and is being produced, but only provisionally named (Hames-García and Martínez 4). This collection includes essays in a variety of topical areas, including gay shame (La-Fountain Stokes), cultural citizenship (Roque Ramírez), concepts of masculinity (Cantú), and an excellent essay by Martínez that looks at Manuel Muñoz's works through the lens of narratology that I will reference in chapter 2.

Although these works have been foundational to jotería studies as a whole, they largely do not offer literary analysis. As González points out in *Retablos*, "At its most compelling, I have given this generation [of gay Latinx authors] attention that it has yet to receive from even the next generation of mariposa scholars . . . who are researching important avenues of thought, though little in the form of literary criticism" (138).[6] That is not to fault these collections for their lack of literary criticism—given the emergent nature of jotería studies, it is more of an indication that there is much work to be done. When literary analysis has been the focus of these studies—we will see examples later—it tends to be conceptualized from a poststructuralist lineage of queer and jotería theory, rightfully considering this production as inherently political given that it finds itself at the intersection of two marginalized groups, queers and Latinx. Nevertheless, and returning to the idea of reader identification that I opened this introduction with, I believe that we can further expand and complicate jotería studies by considering the real-world impli-

---

6. By "next generation," I assume that González means those authors who have risen since the turn of the millennium, including himself, Muñoz, Espinoza, Sáenz, Sánchez, and a number of poets that he mentions. His assessment has somewhat changed since *Retablos* was published in 2013—aside from Martínez's essay on Muñoz that I have referenced, Moya also gives the author substantial treatment in *The Social Imperative*, while Espinoza has been brought up in several academic articles. Nevertheless, despite his expansive literary record, including almost a dozen publications in the last decade, González himself has not received substantial treatment, although a 2014 article by Pérez ("Toward") does look at several of his works in relation to butterfly iconography. Sáenz and Sánchez have yet to receive substantial literary analysis, and I believe that this is because they have both largely written in areas that are critical blind spots—children's and young adult literature. Sáenz has also written a considerable amount of poetry and won the 2013 PEN/Faulkner Award for his short story collection *Everything Begins and Ends at the Kentucky Country Club.*

cations of those *outside* of the academy who are consuming these books and realizing their politics: the reader who picks up these books on Amazon, or at a bricks-and-mortar store like Alvarez did, or even in the classroom.

In conceptualizing the framework for this book, I recalled speaking with Alex Espinoza and Manuel Muñoz and how much they cherish being role models for a young generation of readers, and how much of González's *Retablos* focuses on providing a sense of belonging to those who have not found it within their communities. In short, artists are producing these works for an audience, scholars in the academy inclusive, and they do have real-world implications beyond the sometimes insular theories that we build around them. Exploring this real-world dynamic is critical—as Moya writes in *The Social Imperative*, "unless literary critics attend to the way works can both figuratively and literally 'move' us, they miss something essential about the thing itself" (35), an assertion exemplified in Alvarez's story of discovering *City of God* and why it meant so much to him.

IDENTIFYING SCHEMA

Alvarez's recollection led me to remember my own path of queer literary discovery—borrowing a book at the library during my first year at university. I do not recall the author or even what the book was about, but I can still remember that feeling of titillation of finding it in the stacks, and the perceived danger of checking it out. What if the librarian glanced up, giving me a knowing, disgusted look? What if the bar code would not scan? What if they had to call for help over the PA system, announcing the title just as the cashier did to Dorothy, Blanche, and Rose when they tried to buy condoms in that episode of *The Golden Girls*? Alvarez's example instantly brought back that moment for me as a reader, even if I did not completely share the circumstances.

I would safely guess that many young gay people have had similar experiences in finding that first piece of queer culture—be it a book, a magazine, an obscure television channel, a low-rent movie, or, as a more modern example, a website—that spoke to their identity, particularly when those cultural relics were difficult to find before the wide penetration of the internet. Alvarez's recollection, and indeed my own, shows the power of identification with literature. They could even be considered examples of Phelan's idea of the cultural narrative, a thematic or message that "has a sufficiently wide circulation so that we can legitimately say that its author, rather than being a clearly identified individual, is a larger collective entity, perhaps a whole society or at least some significant subgroup of society" (*Living* 8). Furthermore, he writes that "cultural narratives fulfill the important function of identifying key issues and values within the culture or subculture that tells them" (9). In the context of the United States, Phelan gives the example of the story of triumph over adversity through hard work—essentially, the maxim of pulling oneself up by one's bootstraps (8). This particular cultural narrative is widely recurrent in American popular culture—think of the television series *Breaking Bad*, where it is employed to nefarious and destructive ends—and even informs a good deal of national political rhetoric.

Although Phelan's conceptualization of the cultural narrative is robust, particularly his exploration of how authors employ these cultural narratives and what they mean, his treatment of the reader could be considered heavily theoretical in nature, excessively complicating the dynamic (see 18–20). To deconstruct his argument, I will consider Moya's *The Social Imperative,* which gives reader reaction a more rational role as it turns toward a discussion of schemas and cognition. The idea of the schema is critical in the realm of cognitive narratology, and Hogan's *Cognitive Science, Literature, and the Arts* has been an invaluable resource in making the connection between cognitive scientific studies and literature. Humans, as he explains, categorize "fragments" of experience that are recalled in everyday life—for example, when we partake in the arts (161). This categorization is important for several reasons; as he explains, long-term human memory tends to "cluster" similar experiences and lexicons into schemas, prototypes, and exempla (44)—for example, when presented with the word *dog,* we may envision a general image of a dog, which then may be further delimited as we receive more information.

These fragments of experience, as Moya further explains, are highly dependent on our cultural identification: "The set of schemas any person possesses will be constituted by her bodies of knowledge, her collection of ignorances, her sociocultural biases, and her dispositional attitudes toward learning about new and different situations" (*Social* 24). Illustrating this point, consider a discussion in a recent Latin American literature class about the concept of the ocean. My students, mostly born and raised in central Ohio, far from the cold North Atlantic, considered the ocean as a place of sun and fun. However, for myself, born in rural Nova Scotia and whose family tree is punctuated by death annotations of fishermen "lost at sea," the ocean is an entity to be respected and even feared. In short, my students and I have vastly different schema of the "ocean," something heavily influenced by our cultural backgrounds and experiences.

Keeping in mind the idea of shared cultural signifiers, we can mediate both Phelan's and Moya's concepts to consider the idea of the *cultural* schema. Given that Moya explains the schema as a mental process that informs an individual's worldview, formed by their life experiences, it would stand to reason that like groups would share similar schema, akin to Phelan's conceptualization of the cultural narrative. While all members of that group will not share the exact same set of experiences, the similarities in their life experiences will inform a similar set of schema such that general themes become easily recognizable. Take, for example, the coming-out story, a common trope in queer literature. Although the process of coming out is different for everybody—where, when, how, the level of acceptance received from family and friends—the shared queer cultural schema allows for an understanding of these stories even if they do not exactly represent an individual's experience.[7] In short,

---

7. Schema theory is certainly not new, and as Nishida notes, has been theorized since the time of German philosopher Kant (754). The researcher defines schema generally as "generalized collections of knowledge of past experiences which are organized into related knowledge groups and are used to guide our behaviors in familiar situations" (755), which we can clearly see reflected in the idea of the coming-out story. I add this footnote because Nishida also works with the idea of the cultural schema, applying it to intercultural communication and sojourner's ability for "cross cultural adaptation"

they become identifiable for that particular audience, and it is in that identification that we find the power of the cultural schema. The example with which I opened this chapter—the first-time discovery of queer literature—certainly falls into the same category.

Given that I opened this chapter with a discussion on the importance of genre, the idea of the genric schema must also be explored. What is an identifiable genre or subgenre if not a set of prescribed schema that tie different works together in the eyes of the reader? Genre as a general concept includes categories such as fiction and nonfiction, both of which are marked by certain expectations in the reader, and we can consider the same as true for other subcategorizations such as novella, novel, poetry, the short story, science fiction, literary, romance, children's, and so on. In some cases, this genric schema will manifest itself in a physical form—we all hold a general concept of what poetry looks like, or how long a short story should be—while in others, the content itself will be identifiable. Martín-Rodríguez offers an important discussion of this concept, if not in terms of cognition, in his *Life in Search of Readers,* which I will further discuss in chapters 3 and 4. The author looks at the way that the market has worked to shape Latinx literature so that it is highly identifiable for the potential reader, including the use of pastels on book covers and a bias toward authors who employ magical realism in their narratives. As I will later discuss in relation to Espinoza's *Still Water Saints,* these elements have all become essential to forming the

---

(770). The primary difference in how this book and Nishida look at the cultural schema is that Nishida clearly comes at it from the stance of psychology and interpersonal communication, called Primary Social Interactions (PSI). In sum, Nishida identifies eight types of schema in these situations, which are thoroughly summarized in the article. Although I can see the applicability of Nishida's concept of the cultural schema in this study, particularly for those readers who do not identify with the subject matter of the book (such as a heterosexual audience member reading a coming-out story), we must remember that Nishida's research is connected to in-person interactions, while reading a book is a vastly different experience. A book is a static object—if a reader vehemently rejects or disagrees with its rhetoric, they can put the book down but cannot change what has already been written. On the other hand, the interpersonal interactions that Nishida describes are dynamic: While the schema of the "sojourner" will certainly be affected by contact with the cultural other, so too will the schema of that other.

genric schema of Latinx literature in the eyes of the reader, so much so that the audience has been conditioned to know what to look for and expect from these authors.

In some cases, the genric schema as it relates to content may come to overlap the cultural schema, or even be contained within it. This would probably not be true in genres such as science fiction or fantasy, which depend upon schema that are fantastical and typically outside of the reader's experience. Nevertheless, in the case of gay Chicano literature, it may be difficult, if not impossible, to separate the two. The coming-out story is a hallmark of queer literature generally, and, as noted above, readers may identify with it because it is contained within their own cultural schema. In the wider genre of Latino American literature, magical realism is another important genric schema, and as we will see in chapter 3, given the importance of places such as botánicas, and Catholic mysticism, it presents itself as a cultural schema as well in many cases.

Considering concepts such as the cultural and genric schema exemplifies the divergence between this book and a good deal of work being done in the field of queer Chicanx/Latinx studies, but also shows the importance of multiple lines of inquiry that, through the employment of a broad range of critical tools, cover wider swaths of critical ground. Given this discussion, this book takes the view that through a close reading of gay Chicano texts—those by Espinoza, González, and Muñoz in this case—and by taking into account the sociocultural circumstances from and about which these authors write, we can identify how they challenge, reaffirm, and transform important cultural schema that connect both a gay Chicano community of readers and an audience at large. The intent here is not to imply that only one particular readership can identify with a text; instead, the idea of cultural schema means that particular audiences—gay Chicanos in this case—are more likely to identify with the text given that they likely share a larger number of its embedded schema, but any reader could identify with anything put forth in the work. Although I could theoretically work with any number of authors from this genre, I specifically chose Espinoza, González, and Muñoz because they come closest to what could represent a generational cohort. All were born in the early 1970s and emerged within the same decade—González published his first poetry collection in 1999 and his novel *Crossing Vines* in 2003, Muñoz's *Zigzagger* was released in 2003, and Espinoza's *Stillwater Saints* was published in 2008. Critically, despite the similarity in their respective emergences, they also represent a range of publishing outcomes, a fact that becomes important in chapter 4: González published in smaller and university presses, Muñoz at mid-market Algonquin, and Espinoza at mass-market Random House.

COGNITIVE CLOSE READINGS

Given that this area of research remains underserved, as González himself explains in *Red-Inked Retablos,* each approach—both the structuralist and poststructuralist—serves an important purpose in providing future studies more points of entry into the academic conversation.[8] This expansion also forces us to confront biases that we may hold against certain approaches such as the structuralist-tied close reading, which I will employ at length here. For example, in *Postnationalism in Chicana/o Literature and Culture,* Hernández argues that "it is not enough to focus on close readings of literature or texts . . . when their social context is missing" (2). I tend to agree with this assessment—a close reading absent of social context may be appropriate for a text that is centuries old, but it is insufficient for a work that reflects lives being lived today, particularly in genres rooted in marginalized groups such as queers and Latinx. Nevertheless, the close reading *can* be an invaluable tool, and Moya in particular goes to great lengths to defend its value in *The Social Imperative.*

The goal here is not to reinvent the wheel, particularly given that Moya does excellent work explaining her reasoning, and why the cognitive sciences offer a new path that gives added value to the close reading. She calls upon recent essays by Levinson and by Best and Marcus, who call for a renewed focus on close reading, the first seeing its application both aesthetically and sociologically, and the second advocating surface reading free from political agenda to pre-

---

8. In this way, I refuse to paint either the structuralist or poststructuralist approach as inherently "better" than the other—they are simply different and I have employed both in my research.

vent "heroic criticism" (*Social* 3–4). Given the idea of schema that is forwarded by those working in cognition and literature, the second approach may be virtually impossible, particularly in genres that are inherently political, such as queer and/or Chicanx literature. Nevertheless, to assuage the temptation to accept the author's word as an infallible reflection of reality, Moya reminds us that "a work of literature never represents society as it really is, but rather filters through a literary form the hopes, dreams, illusions, and (sometimes faulty or partial) knowledge of the author about that social world" (8). In short, literature never represents "the truth," but only the truth as far as the author sees it. Keeping that in mind, Moya sees the utility of the close reading as "serv[ing] as an excavation of, and a meditation on, the pervasive sociocultural ideas—such as race, ethnicity, gender, and sexuality—of the social worlds, as well as the worlds of sense, within which both authors and readers live" (9). Moya goes on to explain the usefulness of integrating cognition into the close reading, which I talked about above.

THE POWER OF REPRESENTATION

Importantly, much work done in the field of queer Latinx studies gravitates around issues of representation and where its power lies. For some in the field who examine artistic production,[9] it would seem to lie *within* the artifact itself, given that many of these studies trace how specific representations reflect society and/or cultural practices. For instance, in Soto's *Reading Chican@ Like a Queer*, the author sets out to arrive at the demastry of desire, exploring the "collective circumstances and individual desire, between material realities and interiority—why we love the way we do" (9). She

---

9. Here I specifically separate those in queer Latinx studies who look at artistic production from those who take an anthropological stance. As an example of this, we can look at Juana Rodríguez's *Sexual Futures, Queer Gestures and other Latina Longings,* in which the author examines how said gestures "highlight the everyday labor of political, social and sexual energies that mark our collective will to survive this day" (7–8). Her take, heavily rooted in the political implications of queer gestures, falls outside of the literary scope that I focus upon here.

does this with the ultimate goal of "taking racialized sexuality from a minoritarian to majoritarian position criticizes," ultimately making it "unexceptional" (14), and examines this paradigm in the works of Cherríe Moraga and Ana Castillo, among others. Soto only occasionally moves the conversation beyond the texts themselves—the conclusion where she writes about the politics of Chicanx studies is a good example—and this focus in many ways overlooks the political power that these texts hold beyond their own covers.

In *A Taste for Brown Bodies,* Hiram Pérez importantly criticizes the domination of queer theory by the white and particularly male point of view, considering gay modernity as "inscribed in the nation's imperialist project" (3) reaching as far back as the nineteenth century. He goes on to critically examine this dynamic in the images of the cowboy, soldier, and sailor, and how they "perform colonial labor for a cosmopolitan desire . . . that is fundamental to gay modernity, a desire for the primitive, the exotic, the brown body" (23). Pérez occasionally moves the discussion beyond the representations themselves, such as in his discussion of a screening of the movie *Brokeback Mountain* in Wyoming. In *Homecoming Queers,* Danielson considers *queer* as a verb that means "coming home," particularly that, through creativity, queers come home to their LGBT roots (4). In this way, she examines how "art . . . enables a critical movement toward a reconceptualization of home in language, community, media, and academia" (3), particularly in how artists such as Marga Gomez and Monica Palacios have interpreted their own societal position through their performances. In the final chapter, "Our Art Is Our Weapon," Danielson does begin a discussion about the power of representation and specifically how artist/academics such as Gloria Anzaldúa have encouraged the use of "writing . . . [as] a tool for community and coalition building" (182), but this discussion remains heavily rooted in the academic setting.

These, of course, are only recent works; if we dig back through the history of gay Chicano studies, there are other important scholarly works that focus on the power of representation within the artifact. In Foster's *Sexual Textualities* (1997), the author maintains that in many places in Latin America, the critic must keep in mind that although there is a possibility of same-sex relationships, there is a lack of a "gay" identity, and thus, in many of the works that he studies, he sees a questioning of masculinity instead of the creation of a new identity category (3). In his chapter on gay Chicanos, he furthers this, questioning the homoeroticism commonly seen in the works of Cherríe Moraga, John Rechy, and Francisco X. Alarcón, wherein this concept is framed by mainstream, white society, instead considering them as critiques of gender performance (74–75). Also by Foster, *Chicano/Latino Homoerotic Identities* includes essays on Chicana lesbian writing, poetry, Cuban and Puerto Rican artists, and performance art, among other topics, again keeping the analysis rooted in the texts themselves. His *Ambiente Nuestro: Chicano/Latino Homoerotic Writing* (2006) examines the production of homoerotic writing from a Marxist point of view, looking at the nonromantic issues of identity and how cultural power within communities comes into play in its creation (12), including issues of race, gender, and ethnicity in authors such as Norma Alarcón, Nava, Rechy, and Manrique.

Although they each take different paths, these scholars have offered invaluable insights into the queer Latinx condition, an area that has struggled to gain recognition in the academy. I would like to add to and complicate this scholarly terrain by focusing less on artifact per se and more on issues of reception and audience. Jotería scholarship makes formal what we know on an everyday level: that representations are powerful and that their political potential on the level of the audience is readily evident. I would like to add to the scholarly conversation considerations of how these real-world implications open up a very relevant avenue of study: to provide a sustained analysis of how audiences internalize what they read, and then, critically, externalize onto greater society. The book is a static object—it cannot change—but the reaction of the reader is alive and critical to study.

I would consider this an expansion of the realist position that Martínez advocates in *On Making Sense*, where the author challenges the critic to think *from* the minority perspective, not merely *about* it (4), summarizing his intentions as "show[ing] how the rich and meaningful experiences of racial and sexual minorities can be best gleaned if we assume that there is indeed an objective reality, and that reference to that reality is possible" (5). In short, critics can take a myriad of pathways to theorize concepts of queerness and latinidad, but for real people not taking part in this conversation, these identities have true meaning and value that may have only a tenuous connection to the work going on inside the academy. For example, during our interview, Muñoz shared the rejection of a short story because the publisher did not accept "gay" fiction. This denial was not based upon how the author did or did not interrogate queer subjectivities, or the intricacies of his representations of latinidad, but instead was a swift and brutal rejection of his work because it was gay focused. This, simply put, is the importance of the realist position—identities are real and they do matter, and we find this manifested in both the author and how the reader interprets what they produce.

Despite the divergence of academic discourses outlined on the previous pages, my approach here can be seen as lying at the root of what we do as critics. The product of our academic expertise typically begins as a close reading of a text—we internalize the representation as part of our own schema about the given topic, then externalize it through theory because that is what our profession requires. Jotería scholarship prides itself on this internalizing/externalizing aspect, given its strong focus on turning personal experience into theory. Another strong example is found in late Cuban American queer scholar José Esteban Muñoz's opening to *Disidentifications: Queers of Color and the Performance of Politics*, where he recalls watching a Truman Capote interview on television as a child, at once feeling a repulsion but also "a deep pleasure in hearing Capote make language, in 'getting' the fantastic bitchiness of his quip" (4). Although Muñoz goes on to explore these texts through the lens of identity politics in late capitalism, the internalization of the representation is clear in his work. As he writes about a performance by queer comedienne Marga Gomez:

> Gomez's performance . . . enabl[ed] me to somehow understand the power and shame of queerness. Now, looking through the dark glass of adulthood, I am beginning to understand why I needed that broadcast and memory of that performance [of Capote], which I may or may not have actually seen, to be part of my self. (4–5)

In short, Muñoz, as an audience member, internalized the performances of Capote and Gomez as part of his own schema of queerness, then later externalized them in his academic work. The approach that I take in *Capturing Mariposas* extends such theoretical lines of inquiry along with those works I mentioned earlier. As we will see in each chapter, these approaches each have the effect of identifying particular cultural schema that reflect segments of the gay Chicano experience, much in the same way other critics may employ poststructuralist methods to accomplish the same.

One of the potential criticisms of this study, given that it places the power of transformation with the reader, is the assumption that readers are a monolith that interprets a text in the same way that I do with my trained critical eye. This is a valid critique, but one that I hope to assuage by reading cultural schemas at a broad level. Nor do I pretend that my interpretation is the only way to read these works; while I focus on sympathy and empathy in González's works, it is quite possible that another reader will find those elements most salient in Muñoz's, or will find use of the narration gaps that I employ to deconstruct Muñoz in Espinoza. As with any literary analysis, interpretation is in the eye of the beholder—I looked at the way that these works spoke to me as a reader, how they made me feel, and what they led me to think.

CHAPTER OVERVIEW

Chapter 1 enters into a discussion of two pieces from Rigoberto González's expansive archive: the novel *Crossing Vines* and his autobiography *Butterfly Boy*. Here I look at how the author constructs what I term *affective planes* in order to provoke sympathy and empathy for the characters that he draws in both works. I propose that the author shifts affect toward one character before reversing the narrative flow, but importantly, I assert that *Crossing Vines* is more likely to evoke sympathy and *Butterfly Boy* empathy because of the audiences these works appear to be directed toward. Through these techniques, I believe that González moves toward a cross-cultural/

sexual understanding that challenges cultural schema in order to bring together disparate groups.

One of the most salient features of Manuel Muñoz's works is the idea of playing with the role of the narrator, the filter through which the reader is immersed the storyworld. In chapter 2, I look at how Muñoz constructs the "vague narrator," a storyteller who leaves purposeful narrative gaps that first draw the reader into the story, and then subsequently push them out in a search for meaning and closure when these gaps are not filled. Furthermore, I propose that Muñoz forces his audience to mind read these narrators in order to discern what their true intentions and motivations really are. Many times, this mind reading and gap filling by the reader reaffirms a cultural schema of a hidden and shameful homosexuality, which, if not spoken aloud, somehow does not become real.

In chapter 3, I discuss how Espinoza has seemingly crafted his novel *Still Water Saints* to fit within certain market dynamics that have linked Latinx literature with magical realism. A reader approaching Espinoza's novel would likely expect a magical-realist reading experience given the cover, the reviews, and the first chapter of the novel itself, which tells us that protagonist Perla is a curandera who holds magical powers such as the ability to walk on water. Nevertheless, something curious happens as we advance through the chapters: despite this setup, the author completely deconstructs the idea of magic and that the protagonist can perform it. What we are left with is a magic-*realized* novel that may surprise the reader and transform their schema of what Latinx literature is, and one that in the process recreates a site of magical realism—a botánica—into a space of openness and inclusion. To accomplish this, I employ the cognitive science of surprise and its transformative capability to show how readers assess and reassess plot and themes as they advance through a work.

Within any discussion of genre lurks the idea of commodification, often seen as a dirty word in academia. Nevertheless, confronting this concept in unavoidable: Publishers act as gatekeepers to what sorts of gay Chicano experience we see reflected on the page, restricting their output to what they believe will sell. Keeping in line with the real-world approach of this book, in chapter 4 I look at the commodification of gay Chicano literature to fit into predefined market molds, and the implications of this for how the reader externalizes the politics contained within these works. As we will see, commodification of literature is not necessarily a bad thing, particularly for new(er) authors in nascent genres if it affords them, and their politics, more exposure, and these reader reactions can show us why. As an extension of this discussion, in chapter 5 I let Espinoza and Muñoz have their say through interviews that I conducted via Skype, along with an analysis of González's thoughts through his extensive online interview archive. We explore topics ranging from their creative process to their struggle to be reviewed to their relationship with the wider Chicanx and queer literary communities.

I chose *Capturing Mariposas* as a title for this book because I believe that it best embodies what this books hopes to accomplish—to capture the writing, perspectives, and political potential of these authors. Furthermore, in *Retablos* González asks for more literary analysis of mariposa authors, and here I hope to capture that sentiment. In summary, this book will hopefully represent a strong installment in terms of the study of these authors in particular, and a branching out in the ways that we look at gay Chicano production as a holistic genre.

CHAPTER 1

Can You Feel Me?

Affect and Cross-Understanding in
Crossing Vines and *Butterfly Boy*

IN MY advanced undergraduate class in US Latinx literature, the final assignment was simple: Of all of the literature that we read, tell me what you liked the most and why. I wanted to not only gauge what works I would excise from future syllabi but also obtain insight for this book. Of the works included in *Capturing Mariposas* that I used in class, I expected students to prefer Manuel Muñoz's 2011 novel *What You See in the Dark* over selections of Rigoberto González's 2003 novel *Crossing Vines* given that I believe Muñoz's work to be more interesting from a narrative perspective. Final response papers did bear out this assumption—*What You See* was mentioned by a number of students as their favorite piece of literature from the course. Interestingly, class discussion would seem to have indicated a completely different outcome: *Crossing Vines* generated a far stronger response than Muñoz's work. After rereading both to figure out why this disparity existed, I concluded that *What You See* is the type of novel that readers, particularly those in a literature program at the university level, feel that they *should* like: It is dark and introspective and experiments with narrative forms and timelines. One student described it as "a dark, ambiguous, complex, and mysterious novel," while another wrote that the identity of the narrator is not clear and they were never really certain of the internal motivations of the characters, which greatly added to the complexity of the story. Nevertheless, both did cite it as their favorite work of the class.[1]

Although *Crossing Vines* may not be as complexly constructed as *What You See*, students reacted far more strongly to it as a whole, and to the individual characters in particular. Upon rereading the novel, it became clearer why González's work generated so much discussion: The author frequently uses affect in order to connect characters to readers, which perhaps explains why my students became so protective over the character of Chela, a single mother whose boyfriend frequently skips out on her—students believed that they could *feel* her pain and understand why she was so caustic, or, at the very minimum, feel *for* her pain. The difference in student opinion between *What You See* and *Crossing Vines* may also be explained by Tan's conceptualization of A and R emotions in viewer reception of art. He writes that A emotions are related to the artifact itself and manifest themselves as an appreciation for the work on an artistic level, while R emotions are feelings generated for what is portrayed (120). Given student responses, it could be said that they reacted to *What You See* on the level of an A emotion—an appreciation for the artistry of the novel—while *Crossing Vines* generated far more R emotions, with pleasure in reading derived from the manipulation of emotion in the text, something directed by the author himself.

This manipulation is evident throughout the novel, and notably, it is almost always driven by oppositional characters. Students

---

1. In *Practical Criticism*, Richards warns to exercise caution when considering student responses. The author relates how he presented undergraduate students with a number of poems, devoid of contextual information such as author or title, in order to study "inferior literary response." For him, the analyses of these poems from otherwise intelligent students were startling, as was the variability in their responses. He writes that "it was interesting to observe the wide range of quality that many individual readers varied through. They would pass, with contiguous poems, from a very high level of discernment to a relatively startling obtuseness" (316). For this reason and others, I treat real student and reader responses as a guide rather than a rule.

felt not only for Chela but also for Cirilo, the boyfriend who abandons her and their three children, and I believe this to be due to González's narrator shining a spotlight on each in different chapters. This dual narrative structure also popped up among a wide variety of other seemingly oppositional characters in the novel, and is a testament to the true strength of González's literary technique: the commitment to telling both sides of every story and in doing so, creating an affective plane that readers must navigate throughout the novel. He gives space to Leonardo, toward whom Don Manuel, his father, is rather abusive, but also to Don Manuel, whom we see as being set in his ways and not taking kindly to Leonardo returning home from college and preaching to him about how he needs to be more politically aware.

Although I did not use González's autobiography *Butterfly Boy* in this class, we can see the same sorts of dynamics in play in this work: The reader feels for the grievances that the author has against his father, but, at the same time, also understands how he may be unfair in how he airs them, and how the father may too be worthy of sympathy. Nevertheless, that González frequently evokes affect in his works is not entirely notable; in fact, one could say that it is a rather common trope in literature. Roberts, for example, refers to the novels that she studies as "schools of sympathy" (10) that are designed to make us feel (3), and undoubtedly, this sentiment could also easily be applied to other forms of narrative, including television and movies. What is interesting about González's use of affective planes in both *Crossing Vines* and *Butterfly Boy* is found in how he constructs them and their implications: Through the employment of a regimented narration shift in each chapter of *Crossing Vines*, the implied audience of the novel may be led to feel sympathy for the characters, while in *Butterfly Boy*, the author shifts the affective plane within chapters to create empathy for both the author *and* his father. Both of these shifts are notable because they may work to challenge the cultural schema that readers bring with them, which can also speak to their larger implications in the real world. That *Crossing Vines* likely generates sympathy and *Butterfly Boy* empathy is its readers is a critical component of the rhetoric of these works, which is why I will first discuss these terms so as to establish a framework to move forward.

FEELING WITH AND FEELING FOR

An extensive review of the literature of sympathy and empathy reveals a wide array of at times conflicting findings, and this occurs in studies with origins as diverse as literature, film, psychology, and the cognitive sciences. On a basic level, Keen defines sympathy as feeling *for* and empathy as feeling *with* ("Narrative Empathy" 63), and, if we sort through the various theories and findings, this tends to hold true across disciplines. Wispé, for her part, considers sympathy as containing two actions, the first being a heightened awareness for others, and the second an urge on the part of the sympathizer to take action to alleviate the pain of the other, making sympathy necessarily altruistic in nature (68).[2] I will further consider this altruistic component in chapter 4. Ratcliffe, in a more literary-based analysis, considers sympathy as being nearer to an object, which, in her particular case, is the characters in literature. She also takes the stand that the common usage of sympathy normally includes the idea of empathy, which she defines similarly to Keen (19). In another literature-based approach, Marshall considers sympathy as the capacity to feel the sentiments of somebody else, or, as he terms it, a general sense of "fellow feeling" (3). In the context of his study, based in the works of Marivaux, Diderot, Rousseau, and Mary Shelly, he writes that he finds the term *empathy* to be too vague; specifically, we can-

---

2. Wispé also writes that even though there is an "urge" to help the other, this does not always occur. For example, when reading a book, the reader knows that there is no way to help a potentially sympathetic character. Somewhat more disingenuous is the notion of sympathy leading to selfish helping. Wispé uses the example of a martial arts expert helping out somebody being attacked, not out of a sense that they should help, but rather to demonstrate their prowess (70). In the context of González's works, I believe that we may see this selfish vindication among some of the readers of *Crossing Vines*, who may revel in the suffering of the characters because it reinforces their view that agricultural workers are mistreated or caught in an unjust system. In fact, I believe that the character of Leonardo falls exactly here, and we will later see why.

not know another's pain, so we must "rerepresent" it—a notion that, at least in his conception, necessarily excludes empathy (5).

Carroll, in his study on sympathy in literature, considers it as "nonfleeting care, concern or, more broadly, a nonpassing proattitude towards another person," a category in which he includes fictional characters (173). He continues, explaining that "sympathy, construed as an emotional state, involves visceral feelings of distress when the interests of the objects of our proattitudes are imperiled and feelings of elation, closure, or satisfaction when their welfare is secured" (173), noting that sympathy and empathy may overlap, and a character must be worthy of this proattitude on the part of the reader (174).[3] Eisenberg and Eggum, meanwhile, see sympathy as an "emotional response stemming from the apprehension of another's emotional state or condition"—that is, "sorrow or concern for the other" (71–72) that does not necessarily mirror the emotion that provoked the response. Eisenberg et al. suggest that sympathy stems directly from affective empathy, and indeed may be generated from cognitive processes ("Empathy Related"). Returning to the idea of the prosocial attitude, in "Prosocial Development" Eisenberg et al. suggest that this is the true difference between empathy and sympathy: that sympathy does not create the same personal distress that empathy does, wherein the perceiver is experiencing the *same* feelings as the other. Thus, sympathy is connected positively to prosocial behavior, whereas empathy is not because a feeling of empathy, given that it is likely stronger or more personal, may make the subject want to distance themselves from the other; in other words, empathy is self-focused (647).

---

3. That elation and satisfaction can be considered part of sympathy is a particularly interesting view as many theorists of sympathy, notably Wispé, believe that it only occurs for negative emotions because, as she writes, "sympathizing with another person's happiness . . . would seem inappropriate and insincere" (69). It must be noted that Wispé is, of course, referring to interactions between real people, while Carroll speaks generally of fictional characters. It would be interesting to gauge the difference in sympathetic reactions toward fictional characters and real people, given that we may modulate our responses in front of people who are able to judge us based on those reactions, something not true in the case of reading.

Sympathy and empathy are often explained in tandem because they are perceived to be similar in nature. Nevertheless, just as there is discord in the study of these two emotional responses, empathy itself has been a divided field. More recently, this has manifested itself as division between those who ascribe to simulation theory, more cognitive and motor focused as almost an involuntary reaction, and theory-theory, with more affective roots as something that one has some level of control over. In terms of theory-theory, Matravers, for example, sees empathy as simulating mental states, noting that if the spectator merely "imagines," it falls short of empathy and is most likely sympathy (21–22). The author also sets a test for this mind frame, writing that it has succeeded if the audience is "presumably, not . . . surprised by, or [is] able to predict, fine shades of behavior of the agent" (27). Steuber reiterates the importance of perspective-shifting, here called reenactive empathy (131), in which we "re-enact or imitate in our own mind the thought processes of another" in order to understand their complex behavior (21). Goldie, meanwhile takes a stand against the idea of perspective shifting, instead considering empathy as imaging "how it is" to be the other person (306), not imagining a perspective from inside the other because, as he writes, this stance is infused with "dispositions of character and personality, and with a conception of oneself as having a past and a future in the light of which decisions and choices are made—decisions and choices which one has to live with" (317). Because the other cannot possibly know these factors, they cannot accurately feel exactly what the other person feels but instead can only imagine what it might be like to be that person in their state.

On the simulation theory side, which is generally more empirically based, Hogan's discussion of how long-term human memory tends to "cluster" similar experiences and lexicons into schemas, prototypes, and exempla (44), seen in the introduction to this book, is highly relevant. As he explains, the terms that we read may activate other terms and experiences in our memories (57–58), and we are sensitive to emotional triggers in new experiences. For example, if we feel happy or sad because of this new experience, it is because an emotional memory has been triggered, even if we are not aware of it (182–83). Writ large, experiences or scenes that we read may then activate other clusters of similar memories of our experiences, which is why we are able to "relate" to literature and empathize with characters within those stories.[4]

Other researchers have moved into empirical studies of empathy in literature, including Natalie Phillips, who is performing fMRI studies that scan readers *as* they read Jane Austen (Goldman). Similar to Hogan, Gallese sees empathy as mirroring the emotions of the other on a cognitive and/or motor neuron level (8). De Vignemont, to name one example, differentiates between strong and weak empathy; in the former, the spectator imitates the emotions of others through an automatic motor response, while in the latter, action becomes a model of understanding (183). If empathy is indeed automatic, as the author writes, we would then have to empathize with sometimes conflicting emotions at the same time, which we know does not typically occur (184). On the weak form of empathy, the author further specifies that we may not empathize when expected to (185), some emotions may be easier to share than others (187), the emotion must be strong in order to capture our attention, and it must belong to our past experience repertoire (188), something which Hogan also speaks to.

fMRI neural research into sympathy and empathy seems to reflect the mix of findings mentioned above, although stronger lines have been drawn in more recent studies. Singer and Lamm summa-

---

4. Earlier cognitivist studies of literature, particularly when keeping in mind the views of Hogan, appear to leave little room for sympathy in this discussion. In short, if what we read triggers memory fragments, and it is these fragments that make us feel, whether we are aware of this process or not, we are almost always empathizing to some extent. In my view, we are necessarily feeling *with* precisely because of those triggered fragments, even if our emotional reaction does not mirror the other's. Perhaps this is why sympathy is also referred to as "empathetic concern" in cognitivist circles (see Clark, *Misery* 60). Keen uses the term "broadcast strategic empathy" when referring to how an author may appeal to a reader in terms of universal emotions ("Narrative" 71–72), and I believe that this best encapsulates the cognitivist position at its most basic level—even when a reader reads something that they cannot identify with because it falls too far outside of their experience, they may still empathize because of these recalled fragments that are a part of the reader's lived experience. Nevertheless, as we see with more recent fMRI studies, scientists have located the neural differences between both terms (see Decety and Michalska), which is why I feel comfortable distinguishing between the terms in their use in this study.

rize the wide body of fMRI research involving the pain of others and how the subject reacts to it, explaining that empathy for the other is indeed observable in neural structures, but that it is also a "highly flexible phenomenon" that is changeable "with respect to a number of factors" (81). Among these, the authors raise the question of prosocial behavior, which I will explore more fully in chapter 4. In a 2011 study by Lamm, Decety, and Singer, participants were shown pictures of body parts in painful situations, which activated cranial areas "underpinning action understanding (inferior parietal/ventral premotor cortices) to a stronger extent." They also discovered that employing "abstract visual information about the other's affective state more strongly engaged areas associated with inferring and representing mental states of self and other" (2492). Interestingly, the authors found that these patterns held true "across studies performed in different countries, by different investigators on different MRI scanners, and using different types of paradigms" (2500), suggesting that empathy is hardwired in most humans and not merely cultural in nature.

Unfortunately, there are far fewer studies that look solely at sympathy. Decety and Chaminade, in an experiment in which participants were shown videos of actors telling sad stories as if they had happened to them, found changes in neural patterns, suggesting that "feeling sympathy . . . relies on both the shared representations and the affective networks" (127). However, the authors do mention that their definition of sympathy is "a combination of sympathy and empathy, and reflects at a common sense level how we may in everyday life automatically interrelate with other people" (127). Likewise, much of the earlier literature in this field does not seem to make a large distinction between sympathy and empathy in neural patterns, making a 2010 study by Decety and Michalska a landmark. Here, the authors claim to have found "partially distinct neural mechanisms subserving" the two (886),[5] meaning that, cognitively, we can prop-

---

5. The authors explain that "many recent functional neuroimaging studies confuse empathy and emotion contagion (also called resonance or mimicry) based on the putative mirror neuron system. . . . There is a problem with equating empathy with motor resonance because the latter does not convey insight

erly speak of a distinction between the two terms, which may resolve some of the discord and conflation in this field.

The above studies are not an exhaustive list of the debate between sympathy and empathy, but they do represent a variety of views on this topic. In using these terms, I will heed the words of Batson, who recommends that researchers recognize a schema of difference between sympathy and empathy, and use it consistently (8). To this effect, he outlines eight different concepts of the idea of empathy, and presumably these are the basic schemata that researchers should recognize and employ, whether they label them as sympathy or empathy.[6] Thus, I have decided to return to Keen's summary of feeling *for* as sympathy and feeling *with* as empathy because it appears to best encapsulate the tone of this discussion.

One of the greatest difficulties with applying these terms to reader response in literature is that without performing an empirical study of readers, it is impossible to know exactly what they may feel during the reading process. This is why I have decided to focus on the idea of the implied and represented audience of González's works and how readers *may* react to his writing. I believe, first, that there exists a clear delineation of these roles within both *Crossing Vines* and *Butterfly Boy*, and second, that uncovering these readerships will shed light on why the former would likely generate a feeling of sympathy and the latter empathy. We must also keep in mind that literature is artfully directed by the author—González is the filter through which these storyworlds are created, and it seems that he actively constructs his stories to elicit these affective responses. It is also criti-

---

into another's internal state and does not account for any other-oriented motivational state that characterizes sympathy" (896).

6. Batson's categorizations of empathy are (1) knowing another person's internal state, including her or her thoughts and feelings; (2) adopting the posture or matching the neural responses of an observed other; (3) coming to feel as another person feels; (4) intuiting or projecting oneself into another's situation; (5) imagining how another is thinking or feeling; (6) imagining how one would think and feel in the other's place; (7) feeling distress at witnessing another person's suffering; and (8) feeling for another person who is suffering. The final categorization fits closely with the term *sympathy*, which is also known as *empathetic concern*. See Batson 4–8 for full descriptions of these terms, as well as research that explores them.

cal to move students beyond R-level reactions to texts, deriving pleasure from the manipulation of emotion, into a deeper discussion of the inherent rhetoric of *why* González may have chosen to structure his texts in this way. As we will see in *Crossing Vines*, this may be somewhat difficult to do, particularly given the cultural schema that readers may bring with them before they turn the first page.

SHIFTING ABOUT THE AFFECTIVE PLANE

At its core, *Crossing Vines* is a novel about a community of grape pickers in the Imperial Valley of California (or, as it is referred to in the novel, the Caliente Valley), presumably set around the time that González published it, 2003. There are a number of plot points spread throughout the novel that may resonate with the reader—the threat of the United Farm Workers (the workers in the novel are not unionized, and some adamantly refuse the proposal), the death of former transvestite Moreno at the hands of an overzealous police officer, and a confrontation between the union and the pickers in a grape warehouse, which leads to the shooting of two central characters, Jesse and Amanda.

González has structured the novel in the form of a single day in the characters' lives, beginning at 3:05 a.m. when the grape pickers begin to awaken for their long day of work, and ending at 9:45 p.m. with a brief power outage before bedtime. Each chapter is marked by a different time of the day and roughly the first half of the novel corresponds to their work in the fields, while the second half is far more plot driven, pushed by the events mentioned above. Somewhat unique in the novel is that each chapter focuses on a different character, so by the conclusion, the reader has become familiar with a good number of the workers.

Because each chapter is devoted to a particular grape picker, it is difficult to name a "principal" character, although several do have more than one chapter devoted to them. With this in mind, we can observe how González goes about creating the affective plane that I believe ultimately drives reader responses to the novel as a whole. To use Genette's terminology, the narrator of *Crossing Vines* is extradiegetic, meaning that they describe the experiences of multiple characters in the novel and exist outside of the storyworld, but they accomplish this from a homodiegetic-like (first-person) position, and it is here that we find the function of the affective plane.[7] For example, in an early chapter devoted to Cirilo, the narrator, although remaining in third person, only reveals the internal perspective of that character, while the same occurs with Chela in a later chapter devoted to her. This internal perspective is most times limited to how that particular character may view the world—how they have been treated unfairly, their feelings toward others, and so on, instead of their actual thought processes.

There are, however, a few instances where the reader is explicitly privy to private character thoughts; for example, in the chapter "Chingada," the narrator relates that "Chela straightened up and continued picking, recalling the scene at the daycare center at dawn" (49). Nevertheless, the internal perspective offered by the narrator is generally implicit within the narrative itself. Later in the chapter, the narrator relates that "Chela wanted to be a part of her daughter's schooling but las chingadas teachers all thought the Mexican mothers backwards" (51). The reader may pass this off as being an observation of the narrator, but the strong language used here more reflects the way that Chela speaks—it is not used in Cirilo's chapters. Thus, we see a narrator that at times changes narrative tone based on whichever character is the focus of the chapter, in this example taking on the perspective of Chela, although remaining in the third person. To enter further into the field of narratology, I believe that *Crossing Vines* offers an important example of narrator as focalizer. Some narratologists, Chatman and Prince in particular, see the narrator role as almost entirely objective. Specifically, in Prince's view, the narrator "is an element of *discourse* and not of story"; in short, narrators serve to report and present ("Point of View" 46; see also Chatman, *Coming to Terms* 144–45). Phelan disagrees with this position, writing that narrators do indeed act as lens in the story, even if they are not present in the storyworld ("Why Narrators" 58). He

---

7. See Genette's *Narrative Discourse Revisited* for a more in-depth discussion of these terms.

continues on to list several examples of how focalization through a particular character may be contained within the narrator's own focalization, an argument that appears to rely heavily on semiotics.

Nevertheless, as Bortolussi and Dixon discuss in *Psychonarratology*, much of the argument about focalization is centered upon who "sees" and who "speaks," a distinction many readers may not make (177), making this a discussion almost entirely between theorists of the field. However, I do believe that the distinction between who sees and who speaks *is* important in *Crossing Vines* because of the setup of each chapter. Most readers, particularly those in postsecondary education such as my Latinx literature students, are able to distinguish between first- and third-person narrators as a basic function of a text. *Crossing Vines* differs in that the first page of each chapter gives both a title and the name of a particular character. Thus, after reading through even a portion of the book, the named character immediately produces an expectation in the reader—we know that in a chapter dedicated to Chela, for example, the third-person narrator will shift focus toward her and may embody elements of her speech patterns.

In these cases, Phelan's more recent rhetorical theory of narrative is useful. In it, he describes textual instabilities (between characters) and tensions (between implied authors, narrators, and audiences), how readerly dynamics form in reaction to these, and what judgments readers "are guided to make" ("Voice" 58). In *Crossing Vines*, even though the reader may not be familiar with or understand the concept of focalization, there is clearly a *tension* at play in the narration of the work, and I believe that this manifests itself as the affective plane. The focalization at play in González's work seems closer to what Miall and Kuiken call the spatiotemporal shift, which is included in their theory of aesthetic focalization. They write that this shift has both an internal and external perspective, the first being character based, while the second relies more on the narrator. As the authors explain: "Delimited in terms of a character, a narrator, or even an author's stance towards fictive time and space, this seems analogous to the use of camera position in film" (290). I will now look at some examples of this shift in spatiotemporal perspective in the novel itself, which, in turn, will help to show how González constructs this affective plane.

The reader first meets Cirilo at 4:45 a.m. as he awakens with his friends Moreno, Ninja, and Tamayamá in what is assumed to be a workers' camp. This chapter almost perfectly exemplifies how González uses this spatiotemporal shift both in the formation of these characters and in the construction of the affective plane. As Cirilo prepares himself to eat, the narrator observes: "What bothered him was having to dig into the same undercooked pot of beans from last night. Chela would savor these, his small miseries" (23). Immediately, the reader is confronted with the characterization of Chela as rather vindictive, but with reason—the narrator continues: "Such was her hatred of him for having left her after the birth of each child" (23). Nevertheless, despite actions the narrator describes as "selfish" (23), something akin to a justification is presented to the reader: "Chela couldn't understand why he left each time even though it made perfect sense to him. The first time he simply became nervous and anxious about this child," later adding that Lucita's cries almost drove him to insanity, and that "a solitary wasp of a thought crawled out at the very end: hadn't he witnessed his own father succumb to madness the first months Cirilo's younger sister arrived?" (23). Implanted in the reader is that perhaps it is not Cirilo's fault that he fled, but rather it was an urge that he inherited.

Chela is understandably upset, but does she go too far in expressing it? It is noted that Cirilo does indeed miss his children, and Chela does not let him see them as often as he would like (23). Chela also goes as far as absolutely humiliating him at the birth of their third child, whom she decides to name Mickey, after the Disney character, completing his emasculation (24). When he demands an answer as to why, she snaps, "Because el chingado mouse has more character and certainly more money!" She later goes on to push a nurse "violently" on the bed before storming out of the room (25). At this point, although readers may feel Cirilo to be a negligent father in some respects, do they truly hold him at fault? Chela is certainly not portrayed as a sympathetic single mother—she may be mentally unstable, is prone to violence toward people she does not know, and actively keeps her children away from their father as a form of punishment. Thus, in some way, the reader is able to feel sympathy for Cirilo and his predicament, even in spite of his considerable faults, and may find themselves falling on Cirilo's side of the affective plane, given these emotionally resonant passages that the narrator constructs from Cirilo's internal perspective.

The reader does not meet Chela in person until 7:45 a.m., in the aforementioned chapter entitled "Chingada," a word she frequently uses. The narrator, after building her up as a mostly awful person, immediately begins to soften her, or at least suggests to the reader that she has reasons for being as rough as she is, apart from Cirilo's abandonment of her and their children. It is noted that Chela despises her job in the fields (49), mostly because it takes her away from her children. The narrator also writes that her children face racism at the neighborhood inflatable pool, and she herself encounters scorn when dealing with government channels in the community:

> She was here to prove even the social security workers wrong, but chingado, it was getting harder every year: more restrictions, more paperwork, more cutbacks, and the same bug-eyed secretaries looking down at her as if she'd just gotten off the sofa long enough to walk her overfed nalgas to the welfare office. They treated her like she made those three babies all by herself. (52)

Despite her gruff exterior, which is not softened in any way in this particular chapter, Chela's motivations become more apparent through further details that the narrator offers. She encounters derision and racism wherever she goes, cannot rely on the father of her children, and clearly does not want to be reliant on anybody (54). This is a fairly stark contrast to what the reader initially encountered at 4:45 a.m.—in Cirilo's first chapter—when she appeared almost crazy. Because of the narrator's spatiotemporal shift in focalization, resulting in a corresponding shift in the affective plane, the reader is able to feel for both Chela and Cirilo, even knowing that both have a multitude of flaws. The story of these two characters comes full circle at 7:25 p.m. when Cirilo comforts Chela after the shooting death of cousin Moreno—despite both of their considerable faults, the reader may hope that, somehow, they will find their way back into each other's arms.[8]

---

8. This juxtaposition of oppositional lovers is mirrored in Amanda and Jesse, who work as supervisors to the grape pickers. They are not well liked

The way that González cultivates affect in the reader for both of these characters also recalls Clark's idea of sympathy credits. The author posits that each person has a limit to the amount of sympathy another will provide to them over time—essentially, a credit based upon a myriad of factors. When these sympathy credits are exhausted, no more may be extended.[9] In the example of Cirilo's first chapter, he builds up many "credits" within the reader given what he endures with Chela, but the reader may also subtract credits because he has abandoned her and their children. When we arrive at Chela's first chapter, she may indeed have negative credits, but she quickly builds them up as we learn more about her and her circumstances. This idea of sympathy is also related to justice as we are likely to feel more sympathy for a character that we perceive as just, or deserving of it. As van Peer suggests, whoever is considered more "just" in this situation may depend upon *who* is reading (333), and therefore it may be difficult to gauge toward whom the reader feels more sympathetic.[10]

---

among the workers because they treat them with scorn and derision (45, 50, 71), but, just as in the case of Chela and Cirilo, both receive sympathetic treatments in their respective chapters, which may effectively soften them in the eyes of the reader.

9. Clark's study limits this, typically, to in-person interactions. She writes that a person may build up sympathy credits with others in what she calls their "sympathy biography." She also outlines a number of rules of etiquette for people seeking sympathy, including not "making unwarranted claims to sympathy," not claiming too much, exchanging sympathy with others to keep the sympathy "account" open, and "repay[ing] sympathizers with gratitude, with sympathy, or with both" ("Sympathy Biography" 290). A person reading a novel cannot "exchange" sympathy with a character, but it would be interesting to study this concept more in depth and the limits to the sympathetic union within literature.

10. In van Peer's study, he presented subjects with three versions of the same story, one from the perspective of a wife, another from the perspective of her husband, and a neutral version. From the wife's perspective, she finds the husband inconsiderate when he won't turn down the television volume in order to "have a talk," while from the husband's perspective, he questions why the wife will not leave him in peace. The husband then turns down the volume. A neutral version omits these one-sentence internal perspectives. The husband is considered to be more considerate than the wife, as gauged by readers, in all versions, while the results are mixed in the case of "justness." This suggests that *who* reads is as important as *what* they read—perhaps a single mother reading

Indeed, Chela and Cirilo's final chapter together, where they are sympathetic toward each other, may make the reader feel affect for both.

The other spatiotemporal focalization shift in the affective plane that I will examine is found between Don Manuel and Leonardo, father and son. The fact that Leonardo, a university student who has returned home to do an ethnographic study on his mother, has physically removed himself from the realities of the grape pickers causes much of the friction between him and his father, but as in the case of Chela and Cirilo, the reader witnesses this from two different angles. The reader first meets Don Manuel at 3:05 a.m. as his wife is recording oral histories for Leonardo. The husband sees this as pointless, and does not hesitate in expressing so, noting that "it's a waste of time that's what it is. Idle talk is a waste of time" (7). He then proceeds to pass gas in front of Leonardo, further teasing him by adding, "I saved it just for you" (8). Almost immediately the reader is confronted with what appears to be an earnest son returning home to capture the history of his family, and a father who is, as Leonardo puts it, a cochino (8). In the terminology of Clark, Leonardo quickly builds sympathy credits with the reader as Don Manuel loses them.

However, just as we saw in the case of Chela and Cirilo, the narrator complicates the affective plane when the spatiotemporal focalization shifts at 8:15 a.m. as Don Manuel is at work in the fields. Here, Leonardo comes across as so arrogant and irritating that readers may shift their sympathies more toward his father. This chapter talks about the considerable pride that Don Manuel takes in work, and about how, when he returns home, he wants to simply relax in peace. Unfortunately, Leonardo does not allow that to happen: Bringing home "crazy ideas those Chicano professors had put between his ears" (55), he tells his father that the Virgin de Guadalupe was just a creation of the Spanish missionaries (55), that the farmworkers are being exploited (59), that his favorite program *Cristina* "dulls your brain," and that he should read instead (59). After witnessing the hard work that Don Manuel puts in at the fields, the

---

Chela's account will find Cirilo's actions unconscionable no matter how much the narrator attempts to cultivate sympathy for him.

reader can sympathize with his desire to relax and thus, may understand his outburst:

> Don Manuel yelled out with a burst of energy that made Leonardo drop his book. "I *do*! *I* watch [*Cristina*]. This is *my* house and *my* time to relax and those jototes are prancing around in heels just for me! I don't have the energy or desire to sit around reading books after my long days. You would know that if you knew anything about working in the fields. (60)

Leonardo takes this anger as a sign that Don Manuel should drink herbal tea to calm his nerves, something that will perhaps help him to cut back on his alcohol usage. The final straw for Don Manuel comes when Leonardo suggests that Joaquin Murrieta, considered to be a Mexican patriot by the father, may have actually been Chilean. For Don Manuel, it was "one pendeja too many" and he physically attacks his son (60).

At 8:05 p.m., near the end of the novel, the spatiotemporal focalization shifts again as the reader encounters the first chapter dedicated specifically to Leonardo. Despite the earlier characterization that Leonardo was attempting to tell Don Manuel what was best for him and the other workers, the narrator reveals that "it was a good thing he was studying his parents because he realized how little he knew about them" (201). It is also revealed that Leonardo has struggled with school, which may come across as a surprise to the reader given his apparent studiousness. When he came home, he wanted to impress his family but "had managed to alienate them further" (201). In the next and final chapter of the story, just as with Chela and Cirilo, Leonardo and Don Manuel end the story on seemingly good terms, as the family sits around to listen to Doña Ramona record further oral histories. These two characters are perhaps the most important oppositional pair in *Crossing Vines* because many readers, upon post-reading reflection, may consider Leonardo to be a proxy for the author of the novel for reasons soon to be explained. Nevertheless, I believe that instead of inhabiting this role, Leonardo actually represents what classical narratology calls the *implied reader*, and it is here that we can perhaps uncover the divergent rhetorical possibilities of the novel.

LEONARDO'S SHIFT FROM AUTHOR TO READER

Here I will look at three fundamental areas in regard to how we may process a text: who is writing it, who is intended to read it, and the implicit message, or rhetoric, found within it. In a previous version of this chapter, I explained these roles by way of Chatman's well-known schema (*Story* 151):

However, after attempting to use this schema to analyze a number of different texts in an advanced Latin American literature class, it became clear that students may have a difficult time discerning between some of these roles, and even if they do understand them, they may not be able to apply them to literature. The role of the implied reader and narratee in particular was challenging—in a text such as Hernán Cortés's *Tercera carta de relación,* students were able to identify King Carlos I of Spain as the narratee because Cortés specifically addresses the text to him, but other texts proved unsolvable for them. As Chatman originally noted, some texts do not have narratees (*Story* 150); thus, his schema would move directly to the implied reader. However, as Bortolussi and Dixon explain, many readers feel that the text is directed toward *them* (79) and furthermore, frequently conflate the narrator and the implied author, particularly in cases where the narrator appears to be cooperative (74), which fits the case of *Crossing Vines*.

For these reasons, here I will simplify this schema, taking cues from Bortolussi and Dixon's *Psychonarratology*. When I speak of who is writing the text, I have in mind these authors' category of the *narrator,* which may "consist of information concerning the narrator's knowledge, goals, and perspective" (77), a role that may be conflated with that of the *represented author* (74), something that I believe likely to occur in González's work.[11] Toward whom the text is directed encompasses their idea of the *represented reader,* which may correspond with the real reader in the eyes of many (79). Finally, what I refer to as the implicit message of the text consists of those narrator and author goals that were referenced earlier, driven by the tensions and instabilities in the text. Iser's definition of the implied reader is also useful here, which he describes as "incorporat[ing] both the prestructuring of the potential meaning by the text, and the reader's actualization of this potential through the reading process" (*Implied Reader* xii). The potential of Iser's "implied reader" is powerful, and seems to describe how most critics approach literature—that readers will process texts in certain ways that grasp prestructured meaning as intended by the author. While I also generally follow this line of criticism in this project, with *Crossing Vines* I also attempt to take into account an imperfect readership, such as the students of my Latinx literature class, who bring their own values and beliefs to the text that may hamper their actualization of the "potential meaning."

Given that the narrator of González's work is ever present in the novel, the reader may look to pinpoint which character inhabits this role. Here, the chapter "Coro," the sole chapter in which the spatiotemporal focus shifts toward Leonardo, is critical. The reader already knows that Leonardo has returned to his hometown in order to complete an ethnographic project, based upon recordings that his mother has made for him, but it is the tentative title of this study—*Crossing Vines: A Field Study of the Culture of Work (Grape Pickers Are People Too!)* (204)—that simplifies this search for the narrator. Given that this is the same title as the novel itself, it may be easy to

---

11. As Bortolussi and Dixon write, the *represented author* is not the real, historical author, but instead, in order to "understand the use of a narrator with a given set of characteristics, readers are likely to infer the existence of a creative figure with a set of goals and plans" (76). The authors do believe that in some cases, the *represented author* and the narrator are maintained as distinct entities in the eyes of the reader, particularly when the reader has extratextual information about the author (76). I would also consider this as particularly true in cases where the unreliable narrator is used, as it is here that authorial manipulation of the narrator to specific ends becomes more evident to the reader. It is not likely that this occurs in *Crossing Vines,* however, and readers may easily conflate the narrator with author González.

infer that he is narrating the events in the novel, even though the third-person narration is used throughout. Nevertheless, given that this book is being written as an ethnographic project for a college class, a reader in higher education may not pay much attention to this continued third-person narration—academic essays and studies are usually written in the impersonal.

Interpreting Leonardo as author may also be problematic in that he is a very isolated character within the work; he clearly has limited contact with the multitude of characters whose histories form the vast majority of the stories, with the exceptions of his mother and father. But again, this is solvable, in this case through the narrative device embodied by the tape recorder. Indeed, there is an extensive narration of Leonardo reading the transcription of the tapes, in which Gertrudis, Doña Ramona, Mariana, and Chela all speak. It is noted that these are friends of his mother, whom he has never met (200). The reader is not privy to further transcriptions, but it can be assumed that even if he was not a personal witness to the stories recounted in the novel, they were either recorded or recounted to him by his mother via tape recorder, and he later reconstructed these stories into the novel.

The role of the narratee is also important here, which Keen, who draws from Chatman, defines as the readers to whom the narrator directs their discourse (*Narrative Form* 32). As noted earlier in this chapter, readers in my advanced literature class had difficulty in pinpointing the narratee of a text unless it was explicitly mentioned, and in *Crossing Vines* it is—Leonardo is submitting his ethnographic project to a Chicanx studies professor for review (205). In this case, we would see an alignment of the roles of represented reader and narratee in the professor. In looking at the message or rhetoric of the text, the bracketed title of the work—*Grape Pickers Are People Too!*—may also explain the construction of the affective plane. The title implies that there are people who do not consider grape pickers as worthy of consideration, so it would seem that Leonardo wants to bring some level of understanding to his community and defend them against those who are dismissive of their plight. My own initial reading of *Crossing Vines* indeed took this as the message of the text, as did many student response papers—the bringing to light of the difficult lives of these workers and the system that holds them down. There is certainly much evidence to support this—the long, drawn-out descriptions of the difficulty of working in the extreme heat (84 but one example), which includes one character suffering from heat stroke (104); encounters with and rumors of the Migra (96); and Chela's desire to escape and start anew (23), even though the reader knows that it is not likely to happen.

If this is the case, does the careful cultivation of sympathy in the novel truly matter? Given that the represented reader is a Chicanx studies professor who would likely be sympathetic to these people anyway, the novel/project becomes less about changing minds than reaffirming cultural schema of grape pickers as downtrodden class. An extension of this represented reader would be an audience that shares the schema of grape pickers as downtrodden class, and is naturally more receptive to the sympathy that González bestows upon these agricultural workers. This was certainly true of the majority of the students I taught—humanities majors in the liberal, multicultural classroom who are likely familiar with issues of labor exploitation.[12]

Nevertheless, this reading of *Crossing Vines* may be problematic for a number of reasons, which is why I believe that the rhetoric of the novel differs from what we may at first infer, shifting Leonardo out of the role of represented or implied author and into being the represented reader. Although there is much evidence to support the idea that the novel is about a group of downtrodden workers—essentially victims—*only* considering the novel in this light pushes aside a wealth of textual evidence that counters this. Don Manuel, for example, seems to enjoy and take pride in his job and feels that even simple things, such as knowing the ultimate destination of the grapes he picks, gives his work a purpose (60). In fact, the narrator cites Don

---

12. Vermeule, in *Why Do We Care about Literary Characters*, believes that readers "animate" characters, effectively making them "real," and because of this, may actively seek out allegories in literature. Many critics, such as Kim (later discussed in this chapter), find this conflation with real life to be problematic, but stepping outside of the critical role, we can see many of our students seeking out these allegories, as was the case with my class in *Crossing Vines*. Reader animation of these characters is more difficult to gauge.

Manuel's complaints about Leonardo's way of looking at the grape pickers, recounting:

> Leonardo had built up resentment towards something he knew nothing about. Even worse, Leonardo wanted to educate him about what life in the fields was really all about—exploitation of labor, oppression of the farm worker, violation of workers' rights. Pendejadas! (58–59)

Furthermore, the narrator also gives a sympathetic treatment to both Amanda and Jesse, supervisors, who take a rather dim view of the fieldworkers—"Let them strike. We'll get rid of each one of them if we have to. They're all dispensable, for crissake" (20), says Amanda. Lozano, the owner of the field, whose characterization takes a beating during the altercation with the union at the warehouse, especially after he refers to the workers as "wetbacks" and is called a malinchista (156), is redeemed in a chapter focused upon him, "Shots," at 6:10 p.m. Even the organization that would assuage Leonardo's concerns, the union, is given a rather blurred treatment in the novel. In fact, it would be easy to say that the United Farm Workers Union haunts the novel much like a ghost. A few characters do mention that they would like to join the union, including Doña Gertrudis (72, 73, 116) and Chela (49), but the reader also gets the sense that it is not entirely relevant or effectual. When recounting the atmosphere surrounding the death of César Chávez, the narrator notes that Pifas, a worker, "who had never met Chávez nor was a member of the United Farm Workers Union, couldn't help feeling nostalgic. For what, he wasn't sure" (108). Another worker in the warehouse asks, confused, "Do we still strike in the Valley?" (155). Ultimately, the union's forced entry into the warehouse is treated with a flurry of confusion and chanting that leads to two people being shot (Amanda and Jesse), but it does not appear that this revolt actually goes anywhere or effects any change.

Returning to the idea of who is writing the text, we can assume that if Leonardo inhabits this role, he likely would not focus on those details that may hamper the message of downtrodden grape pickers who suffer from exploitation of labor. Instead, we may be able to consider the use of sympathy in the novel as an indication that the lives of these people are not as black-and-white as somebody like Leonardo would otherwise assert, somebody who, as his father notes, has never worked in the fields (58) and whose resentment may come more from "some crazy idea those Chicano professors have put between his ears" (55) than lived experience. That is not to say that there is not exploitation of labor, or anything else that Leonardo attempts to educate his father about, but instead that the issue is more complicated than this simplistic analysis would indicate—these are real (fictional) people who have a myriad of different issues, including, but not limited to, being single parents (Chela), being sexual minorities (Moreno, Aníbal), worrying about getting enough hours in at the fields (7, 10, 38, 49, 51, 72, 82, 128, 131), making sure their children receive decent educations (52), racism, abusive parents (Jacarinda), aging, and being alone (Don Nico), among other issues.

This point is also strengthened by the fact that González employs a sympathetic narration even with characters that should, if we follow this idea of exploited workers, be perceived as the enemies: Jesse, Amanda, and Lozano in particular. If we return to the title of Leonardo's report—*Crossing Vines: A Field Study of the Culture of Work (Grape Pickers Are People Too!)*—we may come to realize that González's novel is not really about the culture of work of these characters, but instead, and perhaps more simply, about their lives and the various issues they deal with every day. Leonardo notes that one of the goals of his project is to find out "what made [the farmworkers] tick" (202), but it may become clear to readers that although he may put together a report acceptable for a university setting, he truly does not understand them at all because his cultural schema has become far removed from their reality. This point is driven further when, in the final chapter, he continues pestering his mother to record more stories even as she tries to absorb everything that occurred that day, including the shooting of Moreno and the warehouse incident. She finally snaps and knocks the recorder out of his hands (210), which may come as surprising given that she is almost always portrayed as very loving and considerate of his feelings.

In short, as the novel ends, the reader may feel no sympathy at all toward Leonardo, especially given that even one of the most sympathetic characters in the novel loses patience with him. Because of this, in this reflective reading of the story, we can consider Leonardo more in the role of the represented reader—the story is being told *to* him rather than *by* him, in hopes that, through the multifaceted use of sympathy, he comes to understand what really makes these characters tick, challenging the simplistic schema that he has constructed of their lives.

My original reading of this story, and how many of my students also perceived it—that these characters are victims of circumstance—is problematic not only because it ignores substantial textual evidence but also because it denies any sort of agency to these characters. Reader expectations of literature are important to discuss in a novel such as *Crossing Vines*, a work whose readerly dynamics and rhetoric, I believe, are highly influenced by the schema that the audience brings to the experience. That the subjects of the novel are migrant farmworkers is established either by the cover, which depicts people working in the fields, or almost immediately in the first chapter. As mentioned, I taught this novel to a class in a university that, like most, prides itself on multicultural, liberal approaches. Thus, we could consider most of these students as at least sympathetic to or versed in the plight of migrant workers, and as such they would likely bring a number of preconceived cultural schema to their reading of the novel. As Kim writes in the case of Maxine Hong Kingston's *The Woman Warrior*, there is a tendency among such readers to conflate these writings with an entire group of people. This is problematic, however, because "such a reading infantilizes the cultural other and distances the reader's self and responsibility from a problematic situation that *includes* the reader" (104–5).

In the case of *Crossing Vines*, viewing these characters as lacking agency effectively infantilizes them, even if that is not the conscious intention of the reader. Considering the characters of *Crossing Vines* as merely being part of a larger class struggle may indeed put the represented reader, such as Leonardo, or my students, on the side of the characters—we *need* to advocate for these characters because they are unable to it for themselves, casting ourselves and our deeds as altruistic in nature. Kim further explains that in the case of reader reactions to Kingston's work, "such distanced sympathy, rather than empathy, characterizes the reading mode of liberal multiculturalism . . . in which such texts . . . function as . . . representatives in a buffet style approach to discrete, exoticized cultures" (105).

Extending Kim's comments to González's work, I would conclude that what readers feel in the novel is likely this distanced sympathy. Ultimately, this is also what I view as the message that is eventually rejected in *Crossing Vines,* and perhaps over the course of reading the work, the reader would reflect and modify their schema of these characters and people like them, leading to a more empathetic, and less infantilizing, response by the end of the novel. The critical question is if readers actually do grasp the rhetorical possibilities of the novel, or merely take from it the message that fits their worldview. My assumption is that even if readers do not grasp the entire nuance of the rhetoric, a careful reading should not be able to dismiss chapters that demonstrate Don Manuel's pride in his work, as well as the humanization of otherwise antagonistic Amanda, Jesse, and Lozano. I would indeed describe such details as salient features of the novel, emphasized to such an extent that they cannot be dismissed.

While I have not completed an empirical study of the novel apart from in-class responses, cognitive studies have suggested that we tend to be critical of "not true" (fictional) works, even as we enjoy the creation of the storyworld (Cosmides and Tooby 91). Tan, for example, suggests that we frequently go back mentally and reevaluate works, as my students did in their final response papers. He calls this the "law of closure" and explains that it "manifests itself in a search for structure and meaning" (120) even after we have put the work down. In conclusion, and returning to Tan's theory of emotion, *Crossing Vines* appeared to generate R emotions in my students due to the construction of the affective plane and the *tensions* it generated, to use Phelan's terminology, although the true rhetoric of the novel, found in its *instabilities,* may lead to a more A emotion–type reaction in this search for closure.

FEELING FOR EACH OTHER IN *BUTTERFLY BOY*

Although clearly distinct works, *Butterfly Boy* and *Crossing Vines* share much in common—both deal with a community of agricultural workers (González's family, in the case of autobiographical *Butterfly Boy*), the same sorts of interpersonal relationship issues that make *Crossing Vines* an interesting read, and, importantly, significant queer content. In *Crossing Vines,* as noted, both Aníbal and Moreno are queer, the first being homosexual and the second a former transvestite, albeit one who is not gay, while *Butterfly Boy* more or less tells of the author's own path to self-realization. Its chapters are also spliced with sections entitled "Ghost Whispers to My Lover," a person whom the author is desperate to forget. In this section, I have decided to treat the two books as narratives, given that this is how they were written. This is significant because many narratological studies specifically refer to "fiction," a category into which *Butterfly Boy* quite obviously does not fit. Nevertheless, I do consider the book almost fictive in quality—González clearly takes poetic license with his life in the book. This is not to imply that any of the events are exaggerated in any way, but instead that the story is not told in a linear fashion, with cuts to the beginning of his life mingling with his bus ride to Michoacán with his father, and well as the aforementioned letters to his lover.

In fact, when the two works are read in tandem, they can almost be understood as forming one work, with *Butterfly Boy* taking a look at a few of the characters who might be among the workers of *Crossing Vines* whom the reader does not have the opportunity to meet. Another quality that *Butterfly Boy* shares with *Crossing Vines* is González's use of affect in order to capture the reader. Perhaps this is not surprising given that the work could generally be considered a *bildungsroman,* and, as Keen writes, works in this tradition "may have a special role to play in cultivating empathy" through a feeling of injustice (*Empathy* 108). Nevertheless, this feeling of empathy through injustice would appear to be almost necessarily one-directional—in the case of *Butterfly Boy,* that would be toward the young author, whose trials and tribulations we experience in the narrative.

However, just as he does in *Crossing Vines,* in *Butterfly Boy* González constructs an affective plane that primarily positions the author *and* his father at opposite ends of its spectrum for reasons that will become clear. Returning to the idea of the represented author and reader, in the case of *Butterfly Boy* these roles are much less fluid than in *Crossing Vines,* mainly because there is a first-person narration, and we become at times intimately involved with said narrator. However, I do believe there to be two distinct intended/represented readerships of the book, and that this affects toward whom empathy is felt in the narrative. First, there is a queer readership, such as González, the author, and second, a heterosexual one, perhaps with a queer child, like his father. While the first audience would likely be far more likely to pick up this work than the second, I believe that both audiences may be able to feel empathetic to both father and son, although for different reasons.

DIFFERENT EMPATHIES FOR DIFFERENT AUDIENCES

The argument that different audiences will perceive *Butterfly Boy* in different ways—which character we feel *with*—will be buffeted by Keen's excellent deconstructing work found in "Narrative Empathy." After a substantial review of literature regarding the more cognitive findings of empathy in clinical tests, the author's goal becomes uncovering narrative techniques of empathy—how authors invite their audience to feel for the characters they construct, something that frequently occurs with political aims ("Narrative" 83). In this, she is able to pinpoint three techniques in particular, all of which I believe may be applicable to *Butterfly Boy* depending on the intended reader discussed earlier. In general, Keen defines these types as *strategic empathy*, in which an author may "attempt to direct an emotional transaction through a fictional work aimed at a particular audience, not necessarily including every reader who happens upon the text" ("Narrative" 83).

The first such type, *bounded strategic*, many times follows along markers of identity or an "in group," such as gay, black, and so on, but it can also be directed along a plane of experience, such as those who have lost a partner, are a parent, have been married, and so on. Here, the reader either belongs to the in group or they do not, and if they do not belong, the work may not be suited for them. The second type that Keen defines is *ambassadorial strategic empathy*, in which an author may try to write to two groups simultaneously, "hoping to bridge the gap between them" (84). As Keen further explains, this type of empathy "addresses chosen others with the aim of cultivating their empathy for the in group, often to a specific end." Finally, Keen outlines the broadest type of empathy, *broadcast strategic*, which calls upon readers to identify with "common human experience, feelings, hopes, and vulnerabilities" (85). As the author writes, this type of empathy is often derided by critics exactly for being too broad, and perhaps simplistic, but it is also easy to see where this can come into play in any number of narrative works, where the reader may identify with a character based upon a particular emotion they feel at a particular moment. However, before entering into the discussion of how these concepts apply to González's work, I will examine how the author constructs this affective plane to lead the reader to feel with both himself *and* his father, challenging cultural schema in the process.

HOW FLAWED INDIVIDUALS DRIVE EMPATHY IN *BUTTERFLY BOY*

As already mentioned, *Butterfly Boy* differs from *Crossing Vines* in that González is narrating his own life from the autodiegetic position. Because of this, at no point in the work does the reader witness anything that the author himself was not privy to, including the thoughts of others. The reader is thus more naturally inclined to feel with González, if he shows that he "deserves" such sentiments. And indeed, I believe that he does, and that this is evident from the very first chapter, where he recounts his relationship with his boyfriend. Effectively, the author invites the reader to *feel* with him—he primes the text to elicit these emotional responses as the entire chapter is a juxtaposition of the schizophrenic moments of an abusive relationship where González is the victim. This culminates in the author storming out of his lover's apartment, knowing that the relationship is over, and I believe that the use of descriptive words here works to open the reader to feeling for the author along a cognitive standpoint. He writes:

> "I'll walk back to my apartment," I say.
> "I wasn't offering a ride," he says. I feel the sting all over. And then comes his dare, "Is something holding you back?"
> . . .

Out of habit I'm about to say, "I'll call you later," but I hold the phrase just in time and it drops like a weight inside of me. (6–7)

In particular, the descriptive phrasing of "sting" and "drops like a weight inside of me" may take any reader back to the end of a relationship, where words become arrows intent on damage.

With the reader primed to feel with González, further events in the work may elicit even stronger affect, particularly the death of the author's mother, especially given that at the time, he is a child who does not seem to fully understand what death means. At the funeral home, after a lady tells González that his mother is now asleep and waiting for God, he takes a closer look for himself, indignant that nobody really knows what she looks like when she is sleeping. Suddenly, the author sees foam bubbling from her nose. He writes:

"Look! Look!" I shouted. "She's moving!"
. . .
"Is she alive?" I asked, but no one heard me. . . . After a brief and subdued commotion, small pieces of white cotton had been stuffed into my mother's nostrils. I looked on in horror. (109)

While this passage may be more affective for somebody who has lost a parent, or has tried to explain death to a child, it is difficult not to feel for the young author in this moment, when he suddenly gets a very real lesson as to what death means.

Aside from these passages, readers are invited to feel for the author when he describes the poverty he suffered in Zacapu, his hometown in Michoacán, after his father left to return to the United States. He recounts:

We were going hungry. A person who experiences hunger never forgets that feeling. It is more than emptiness, more than an ache at the center of the stomach—it is a waking up and going to bed with shame, as if this stiffness of the jaw and the hardening of the belly is part of some punishment. The flesh begins to feel transparent, and a strange echo resounds in the room when you admit to your weeping mother that you want real food, not tortilla with cheese and hot sauce, which she's been feeding you the entire month. (52)

Instead of simply writing that the family was going hungry, the author instead attempts to draw the reader into the world of personal famine, and although the average reader likely cannot approximate that feeling, González may bring them closer to doing so.

The above passages could very well draw any reader into feeling with the author, but given that the work is heavily queer focused, I feel that it would have particular resonance with that audience. *Butterfly Boy* is not just an autobiography about a poor young Mexican American boy who frequently migrates across the border with his family; it is also about how he comes to terms with his homosexuality and what the perception of this is in his family, where he is still closeted. This situation would likely create a strong sense of Keen's bounded strategic empathy among many queer readers, who have likely had similar experiences in coming to terms with and exploring their own sexualities, as I discussed in the introduction in terms of the coming-out narrative. This is particularly true in passages that deal with the author as a child entering adolescence and being confronted by an ingrained homophobia. In one passage, he is mercilessly teased by his cousins and brother because of the affectionate relationship between him and his mother (62) and called a maricón and sissy because of his high-pitched voice (90). After this incident, he wonders if he had been meant to be born female, writing:

> I wanted to be a girl because I wanted to do girl things: comb my long hair, sit on the back of the pickup truck and whisper secrets, and wash dishes and stick my tongue out at the boys when I caught glimpses of them playing ball through the window over the sink. All the boy activities just seemed like too much work. (91)

Apart from simply wanting to perform these female-coded actions, he actually does on a number of occasions. In one scene, as he is playing with rag dolls he has created out of bandannas, his brother comments to their father: "He's so stupid. . . . Look at the stupid games he plays." González is quickly admonished by his mother, even though he insists that they are not dolls, but snakes (94–95). Another time, the young author decides to walk out of the bathroom with a towel wrapped around his head, turban style. He recalls:

> I had no idea I was doing anything wrong because I had seen my mother do this every night. I liked the way a few damp strands of hair stuck to the skin of her nape and forehead. . . . My waltz had been carefully choreographed from the bathroom to the living room so that everyone in the house got to see me. (95)

However, soon after stepping out of the bathroom, his mother yanks the towel off of his head and punishes him with his father's belt (95–96). Again, this is another scene that is primed to resonate with a gay male audience—being punished for transgressing gender roles—although it may be difficult to make this assertion without falling into stereotypes or explaining to a heterosexual audience why wrapping a towel around one's head may seem like a glamorous thing to do.

As with *Crossing Vines*, it is important to consider the cultural schema that readers may bring with them to *Butterfly Boy*, and how these may be changed by the instabilities and tensions found within the text. As discussed earlier, this work would likely attract a gay male audience, perhaps Latinx, because it speaks to them as readers, like a number of González's other works.[13] While I do not want to enter into a discussion of stereotypes in Latinx communities, we generally know from a wide variety of literature that LGBT Latinx, and indeed queers in general, often have problematic relationships with families who are not accepting of them or are outright homophobic. Thus, the reader of *Butterfly Boy* likely comes into the work with that particular cultural schema in mind, expecting those sorts of textual instabilities between the protagonist and other members of his family and community. González himself feeds into this expectation on the page before the body of the autobiography:

> Of curse I love my father.
> —typo in an email to a friend

---

13. A few other works of González's that feature queer content include *Men without Bliss* (2008), a set of short stories with several gay Chicano protagonists, as well as *The Mariposa Club* (2009), *Mariposa Gown* (2012), and *Mariposa U* (2014), adolescent-oriented novels about growing up gay and Latino.

> Children begin by loving their parents; after a time, they judge them; rarely, if ever, do they forgive them.
> —Oscar Wilde

This artful direction by González may lead the reader to believe that the author has problems with his father, even before the work has properly begun, and, given the context of the autobiography, we can assume that it is because he is gay and his father is homophobic and unable to accept his son's sexuality.

Nevertheless, what is perhaps most interesting in *Butterfly Boy* is that González does not allow himself to wallow in self-pity. Despite the hardships that the author recounts, he is also quite critical of himself, particularly when it comes to his interactions with his father, and this is where the reader must navigate the book's affective plane. The two have a very contentious relationship, and a good deal of this stems from his father's alcoholism, his abandoning of teenage González and his brother after the death of their mother, and his father's perceived offense at the author's effeminacy. The reader first encounters this friction soon after González returns home from Riverside, where he studies at a university, and immediately confronts his father about a ruined picture of the father and his mother. González viciously attacks his father about the picture, to which his father responds: "Why don't you shut up? . . . What happened to this photograph hurts me much more than it does you" (15). Perhaps to the surprise of the reader, the author immediately backs down, writing that "I feel as if he's kicked me in the stomach because I know it's true. . . . I'm like a child in a tantrum. . . . Why don't I feel that level of rage for [my boyfriend]? Why am I so cruel to everyone else?" (15). As this scene demonstrates, unlike in *Crossing Vines,* the construction of the affective plane is not regimented by chapter, but rather exists *within* chapters, with the effect of creating a more natural narrative. González effectively draws empathy toward himself, then turns and reflects it toward his father, often at a cost to how readers may perceive the author himself.

González's willingness to paint himself in a negative light also surfaces on the bus ride with his father to Michoacán from Indio, California. He notes, at different points, that he ignores his father's attempts to make small talk (23); fakes politeness with him (30);

treats beggars with disdain, for which his father scolds him (29); treats other passengers on the bus as nuisances (103); and talks of how much he wants his father to "go away" (105). From what González recounts to the reader, his father truly attempts to connect with the author on the bus ride: He establishes a paternal role in making sure that the author has food to eat (33), says that he just wants his son to be happy and smile more often (35), and allows his son to rest on him in order to fall asleep (36). Despite their difficulties, González appears to have a great admiration for his father—he recounts how they bonded over sci-fi movies and how his father was obsessed with UFOs (38–39), and how his father was a local singing sensation in Michoacán (17–18).

Returning to the theme of the author's gender transgressions, there is one particular scene that I believe best illustrates the two potential intended audiences of the work, and how empathy is directed by the author. Through a number of these scenes occurring during his childhood, González writes how, despite being "effeminate and demure" (88), he attempted to exert a more masculine persona around his father, including cursing when he hurt himself, playing with his brother's action figures, and talking about soccer, despite the fact that he hated sports (88). Interestingly, for his gender transgressions, it was almost exclusively his mother that punished him, such as in the towel incident described earlier. He recounts that "I learned quickly that my mother's actions were not necessarily meant to protect me, but to protect my father. My father didn't beat me for being a sissy, but I knew it bothered him greatly, so it became my mother's responsibility to censor and punish me" (95).

This passage may demonstrate how the reader never truly gets a sense that his father is actually bothered or ashamed by his son's actions, but rather does not know how to react to them. This is evidenced a few pages earlier when the author, home alone, decides to experiment with his mother's clothing and nail polish. When his father walks in, the author is, of course, expecting perhaps violent reaction. His fear is palpable:

> There I was, his firstborn, his namesake, experimenting with fingernail polish. I froze up, hoping I'd become invisible. I tried to trigger a seizure but my brain went numb . . . the panties crawled down my

arm and caught at the elbow. My face burned with fear. All I saw were my father's eyes growing in size and intensity as he took in the whole living room without blinking. Would collapsing at his feet begging for mercy help? It was worth a try. (92–93)

This humorous reflection is likely something that would generate a significant amount of bounded strategic empathy among the gay intended readership, who may share like incidents as part of their cultural schema, but I believe that his father's reaction is perhaps even more important. To the author's surprise, his father says nothing and goes to the bathroom, only coming out after a sufficient amount of time has passed for the young author to clean himself up. After that, the father still says nothing, instead cooking dinner while the author plays with the father's guitar (93).

Here, I believe it becomes clear that there are indeed two intended readerships of *Butterfly Boy*, a queer one, which is more obvious, but also a heterosexual one, perhaps parents or relatives or kin of queers who have found themselves in similarly uncomfortable situations. Although González does have legitimate issues with his father, it is also clear in the work that he does not seem intent on portraying him as a monster, but rather somebody who has made some poor choices and does not always know how to deal with more sensitive topics, such as his son's homosexuality or the death of his wife. Nevertheless, González clearly still loves and admires his father in spite of his faults. Thus, this secondary intended readership would likely not feel guilty for empathizing with the father, finding him worthy of such feelings, and may indeed find themselves in a bounded strategic empathetic relationship with him, based upon shared experiences of not knowing how to react to their child/relative/friend's homosexuality or experimentations.

If we continue to follow Keen's logic, and because the author has put much work into making both himself and his father flawed, yet empathetic individuals, it would stand to reason that there would be cross-empathy among the intended readerships, working to challenge the cultural schema of each. In fact, I believe this cross-empathy—getting the reader to, in the words of Keen, "feel with the alien other" ("Narrative" 83)—is one of the successes of *Butterfly Boy*. A gay readership may very well feel empathy for the father in an ambassadorial-type scheme, while a straight readership would likely feel the same for the author. In this type of empathy, writes Keen, the author may try to write to two groups simultaneously, "hoping to bridge the gap between them" ("Narrative" 83). Ultimately, I believe that is what González attempts in *Butterfly Boy*: to show homosexual readers that their parents/relatives cannot be perfect and need time to deal with deeply ingrained homophobic tendencies, and to give insight to heterosexual audiences on what it is like to grow up "different."

It is likely that writing *Butterfly Boy* was a cathartic action for the author, and reading it may very well be for its audience, too. In a general sense, Scheff summarizes the theory of catharsis as "thrill-seeking [as] an attempt to relive, and therefore resolve earlier painful experiences which were unfinished" (13). Certainly, in the case of González as author, it is easy to see how writing this work would be cathartic. However, Scheff also describes how drama can be cathartic for audiences, specifically that we may cry over the fate of Romeo and Juliet in order to relive "our own personal experiences with loss" (13). If we accept this to be true, then *Butterfly Boy* can also easily be understood as a cathartic read for these two intended audiences. If we consider the audience referenced earlier that is most likely to pick up this work—the gay male audience—perhaps there is a didactic lesson to be found here, as in *Crossing Vines*. Even though González primes the reader to expect his father to be portrayed in a certain way, the construction of this affective plane may challenge particular cultural schemas, opening their minds to their own families, or queer relatives, and reevaluating these relationships. In turn, I believe this becomes the hopeful message of both works—mutual understanding and learning to bridge sympathy and empathy gaps between divergent groups.

CONCLUSION

It some ways it is difficult to speak of diverse readerships in works such as *Crossing Vines* and *Butterfly Boy* because they have not appeared on a best-sellers list, and there is little internet chatter about them. Thus, while we can speak of the theoretical implications of these works, in reality, they likely do not hold that much sway. This idea of a political function of these works is something that I will discuss further in chapter 4, where I focus more upon how the reader may externalize what they have read. Nevertheless, even minor works do have an important role to play in changing individuals' perceptions of disfavored groups such as migrant workers and gays. Perhaps the importance of a work like *Crossing Vines* is to capture readers who have or may have sympathy toward these characters and their real-world counterparts and transform this into empathy—effectively peeling away the infantilizing rhetoric and replacing it with a realization that these characters (and people) do possess agency and are worthy of respect, not mere pity. The role of *Butterfly Boy*, meanwhile, could be to sway readers to reevaluate their own relationships, realizing that nobody is always a victim or a villain. I believe that González may indeed accomplish these important goals in his works, if, importantly, readers pay attention to evidence that may conflict with their cultural schema and be willing to accept the transformational rhetoric that the author puts forward.

CHAPTER 2

Sexual Shame

Bridging Muñoz's Vague Narrator

FROM A narratological standpoint, Manuel Muñoz could easily be considered one of the most interesting voices in Latinx literature. By and large he is a literary experimenter, producing twisty narratives that frequently require the full attention of the reader in order to discern the motivations of the characters, to follow how the various plot strands weave themselves together, and many times to understand the narrator role itself. When I first dove into the titular story of *Zigzagger*, I freely admit to rereading the text several times in order to fully understand what was happening, and stories like this pop up through his works. For example, various narrators in that collection refuse to give names to characters ("Zigzagger," "Campo," "The Wooden Boat"), while others address the reader directly, using the second person. *The Faith Healer of Olive Avenue* is much more traditional in its approach, but *What You See in the Dark* again plays with this role, opening and closing the novel in the second person, but using the more common third person in the intervening chapters.

The exercise of rereading "Zigzagger," and indeed several other stories across Muñoz's works, proved invaluable once I began to consider what the text was doing to me as a reader: pulling me into the story, then pushing me out in a search for closure, much like I discussed in relation to Tan in chapter 1. My need to reread the story occurred precisely because I felt that the narrator had purposefully withheld key story pieces that I needed in order to fully understand the text. I have decided to call this the vague narrator—one that opens narrative gaps in the text in order to trigger reader arousal, but does not resolve them, leading us to reevaluate the story itself. Because this narrator pops up several times, particularly in his two short-story collections, the audience may be led to mind read the narrator as if they were a character in the text in order to discern their motivation for withholding these narrative pieces. In this search for closure, the reader may uncover the affirmation of a cultural schema common in several of Muñoz's stories: a shameful and hidden homosexuality that, if not spoken aloud, is somehow less real.

To be clear, this does not happen in all of Muñoz's works, but rather in several of those stories where Muñoz challenges the audience to read the narrator as if they were another character. Here I will consider a number of his short stories in order to examine this pull and push, how these narrative gaps arise, and how we arrive at the larger cultural schema of the text itself. That Muñoz toys with the role of narrator is not unique to his writing, but because many narrators in literature act as mere reflectors of the story, experimentation with the role tends to draw immediate reader attention. First, I will look at the typical role of the narrator, and then at what happens when this aspect is twisted beyond what we normally expect.

NARRATING THE NARRATOR

The role of the narrator has engendered a wide breadth of studies within the field of narratology—too many, in fact, to be able to fully summarize here. As we saw in chapter 1, in Narrative Discourse, Genette distinguishes between a series of narrator positions based upon who is telling the story and where they exist in the storyworld, including the extradiegetic and homodiegetic. Booth, meanwhile, looks at distance between the narrator and the implied author

(156)—a term he coined—as well as the idea of the unreliable narrator. As Prince observes, the narrator "is responsible for the shape and tone of the story" ("Introduction" 8) and "more or less explains the world inhabited by his characters, motivates their acts, and justifies their thoughts" (15). In the previous chapter we also saw Chatman's scheme of the "narrative communication situation" (*Story* 151), which includes the roles of the implied author, narrator, and narratee, among others. This is just a small sample of the work done with the narrator role, and what many of these studies have in common is that they approach the text on an almost semiotic level that at some point may lose connection with average readers. Bal, who writes of the layers of narration of narrative, story, and fabula, explains that the "analyst . . . distinguishes different layers of a text in order to account for particular effect which the text has upon its readers. Naturally, the reader, at least the 'average reader'—not the analyst, does not make such a distinction" (6).

Because this study is interested in real readers and how they internalize the narrators that Muñoz constructs, I have taken interest in Bortolussi and Dixon's *Psychonarratology*, which considers narratology from the empirical perspective of reader response.[1] The authors believe that readers recreate the narrator as if they were a conversational partner (60), that the reader's perceptions of the narrator and the author likely overlap (74), and that they perform a narrator analysis through explicit attributions and inference invitations. Explicit attributions occur "when characteristics, behavior, knowledge, or beliefs are attributed to the narrator explicitly in the text" (80), while inference invitations "pertain to what is *not* said about the narrator and consist of those signs and signals that invite the reader to make inferences beyond what is stated in the text" (81). In the authors' example, an ironic tone may suggest that the narrator harbors disdain for the characters, even if they do not explicitly say so. When narrators exist in the storyworld as a character, their thoughts are readily available to analyze, but this may not be

---

1. These authors also give a more in-depth overview of research into the narrator, some of which I have touched upon here. See 61–73 of *Psychonarratology*.

the case with third-person narrators. Here, the authors suggest that readers may associate this storyteller with a particular character that has privileged status, especially if the narrator provides "detailed information about that character's thoughts, feelings, perceptions, and behaviors" (82). Ultimately, the authors believe that this may lead to a transposition in the mind of the reader between character and narrator, which I find problematic in some sense given that in many cases, we encounter omniscient narrators that have access to the thoughts of multiple characters.

In this vein, we could consider Alex Espinoza's *Still Water Saints*, which I will look at in the next chapter. The reader may identify the narrator with protagonist Perla, but there are also many chapters where she exists only as a background character, troubling this transposition. In that novel, just as in many narratives, it is likely that the reader does not consciously take note of the narrator because there is little reason to do so. The fluid role of the narrator is perhaps best summed up by Stanzel, who writes that "the narrator . . . can either perform before the eyes of the reader and portray his own narrative act, or can withdraw so far behind the text that the reader is no longer aware of his presence." He calls these the personalized narrator and the "invisible, unpersonalized stage manager behind the scene" (17).[2] Many of the stories in Muñoz's *Faith Healer* contain a straightforward narration where who is telling the story is simply not that important. This usually occurs with third-person narrators who withdraw into the text, whose function is found in introducing the reader to the characters and moving the plot forward, not giving the reader any reason to question their role or to consider them as an independent entity. For example, in the story "Lindo y Querido" from *Zigzagger*, we meet Connie, a housekeeper whose son was recently killed in a motorcycle accident. The narrator of this story builds the plot through carefully placed narration gaps, but eventually does resolve the action, revealing that Connie's son died in an accident with his boyfriend.

---

2. Although perhaps invisible, Stanzel does consider the narrator's voice as "always audible," seeing them as the mediary of the narrative (4).

What is of interest here are the narrators that Muñoz constructs that the audience must confront, and how they first pull the reader into the story and then subsequently push them out in a search for closure. To obtain this sense of narrative satisfaction, I propose that many readers are likely to mind read these narrators in order to discern their true motivations, taking into account both the explicit attributions and inference invitations within the text itself. However, before entering an analysis of these stories, I will look at the concept of mind reading, how it has proven useful in literary studies, and how we can extend it to the narrator role.

MIND READING THE NARRATOR

On a basic level, theory of mind (ToM), also known as mind reading, attempts to explain how humans manage to gauge each other in day-to-day social interactions. As Mitchell reminds us, "we are not capable of ESP" (3), meaning that we do not have direct access to the thoughts of others, and thus the importance of ToM is found in explaining how we may believe that we know what another person is thinking. As Mitchell further explains, "we can make an educated guess by observing what other people have or have not seen, and assume that what they think will be based on this" (6). To demonstrate this, he uses the example of somebody being given a box of chocolates and explains that this person will believe that the box contains chocolates because they have no reason to assume that it does not. However, if chocolates are replaced with bananas the receiver of the box will still believe that they are chocolates until they are opened and the switch is discovered. As outside observers, if we witness this scene in its entirety, including the replacement of chocolates with bananas, we take into account both actions: that the receiver will still believe that the box contains chocolates because they would have no reason not to think so, but also that the box does indeed contain bananas (Mitchell 3).

Nevertheless, attributing ToM is not always as passive as in Mitchell's example. Consider an expression such as "I know what you're thinking," which implies an interaction between speaker and receptor. Unless the other party reveals exactly what they are thinking, we really do *not* know, because we have no way of accessing their inner thoughts. We can, however, read their behavior. Here, Mitchell uses the example of how people attempt to make themselves attractive to somebody else (6). The person attempting to be more appealing may try to read what the other finds attractive, perhaps through their reactions to others—in effect, mind reading them—and adjust themselves accordingly. Mitchell notes that ToM is particularly useful in communication, where appropriate interactions depend upon the accurate assessment of the speakers' motives (7). Zunshine, one of the most prominent scholars of the study of ToM in literature, describes it similarly—attributing behavior to underlying mental states, something we do automatically and in context—and further positions it as our endowment as a social species (*Why We Read* 8).

ToM has proven particularly fruitful in cognitive psychology, particularly in regard to how and at what age it develops, and when it does not.[3] It has also more recently been applied to literary studies

---

3. The first study that produced the term *ToM* did not examine human subjects, but rather cognitively capable animals. In "Does the Chimpanzee Have a Theory of Mind?" Premack and Woodruff theorize: "An individual has a theory of mind if he imputes mental states to himself and others. A system of inferences of this kind is properly viewed as a theory because such states are not directly observable, and the system can be used to make predictions about the behavior of others" (515). As Leverage et al. explain, Premack and Woodruff concluded that chimpanzees do indeed possess ToM based upon their results. Soon after, the study of ToM moved to humans, where there would be much more interest in the topic due to practical implications (3), such as at what age ToM develops and what its ramifications might be. Empirical studies by Wimmer et al., for example, generally cite age four as the time "when children begin to consider systematically the other person's informational accesses in the assessment of the other person's knowledge" (189). In other words, it is at this age that children begin to perceive the difference between their knowledge and that of others. The gap, at least for these researchers, was found between being able to perceive this difference *and* being able to detect "poor quality of informational sources," which occurs at age six (191). In connection to human development, some of the most practical implications of ToM have come in the study of autism. Baron-Cohen et al. found that autistic children fared quite poorly in tests involving mental states, even worse than children in the study afflicted with Down syndrome. Carruthers summarizes the field, explaining

in its more abstract definition—the "contemplation of other's intentions, motives, beliefs and attitudes" (Mitchell 11), instead of in the highly visual manner of those who originally studied it in chimpanzees and autistic children. In literature, ToM manifests itself in how we may read the intentions of others through what we perceive on the written page—how the body gives up the true state of characters' minds. In short, as Zunshine explains, the body becomes the text that we "read," making assumptions about characters' mental states ("Theory of Mind and Michael Fried" 185). In her influential *Why We Read Literature,* she explains that this "mind-reading" is pushed to the boundaries of its capabilities by literature, "testing" our ToM competence, and that our cognitive rewards for taking part would be similar to those of pretend play (17). Furthermore, she believes that this "test" keeps us pleasantly aware that it is running smoothly (17). For example, we may read a certain character as being in lust with another through their corporal actions,[4] and if this is later confirmed as true, we receive our "reward"—being correct, which may increase our satisfaction with the text itself.

Zunshine writes that we are able to do this because of "cognitive slippage," meaning that, at least during the moment of reading, we do not distinguish between real and fictional people (*Why We Read* 19). In other words, we may become so immersed in a work that the world created within it becomes "real" for us, at least in the moment we are reading it, meaning we read the characters as real people.[5]

---

that scholars such as Leslie and Baron-Cohen, across their body of work, argue that "autism should be identified with *mind-blindness*—that is, with damage to an innate theory of mind module, leading to an inability to understand the mental states of other people" (257). Carruthers believes that this is also reflexive, meaning that people with autism "might have severe difficulties of access to their own occurrent thought processes and emotions . . . they do seem to have difficulty in introspectively knowing what their current thoughts and emotions are" (261).

4. Zunshine calls this reading of bodily states "embodied transparency." See "Theory of Mind and Michael Fried" 202; "Theory of Mind and Fictions" 70.

5. In *Why Do We Care about Literary Characters,* Vermeule believes that readers generally "animate" characters in literature, but also deanimate those who have negative qualities, such as killers (26).

This can be a point of conflict between average readers of a text and more serious readers such as critics. While the former group may look at a text on a higher level—appreciating aspects such as narrative construction—it is suggested that most readers are likely to enjoy a work of fiction precisely because of this "slippage." We want to know what will happen to the characters that the author sketches, if the villain will get their comeuppance, if the hero will prevail, or if the star-crossed lovers will finally be united after their many trials. The examples that authors such as Zunshine, Mitchell, and others give are innumerable, but all work on the assumption that we will animate the characters in some way that is not necessarily written on the page and that, many times, the author forces the reader to do this in order to understand what is happening (Oatley 15). As Oatley suggests, ToM "is a requirement to understand this kind of narrative" (15) because it builds out scenes in our minds.[6]

Going further, in *Fictional Minds*, Palmer theorizes that readers may "create a continuing consciousness out of the isolated passages of text that relate to a particular character" and assemble these perhaps diverse pieces together into an "embedded narrative," which includes "the whole of a character's various perceptual and conceptual viewpoints, ideological worldviews, and plans for the future considered as an individual narrative that is embedded in the whole fictional text" (15). Combined with Bortolussi and Dixon's idea of

---

6. While theorists of ToM may have been somewhat critical of more structuralist forms of narratology (see the introduction to Palmer's *Fictional Minds*), there have undoubtedly been criticisms of ToM as well. Although the anthology *Against Theory of Mind* does not specifically delve into literature, editors Leudar and Costall are concerned that "there exists not one single published response in which proponents of 'Theory of Mind' address systematically and carefully the objections to their programme" (1). Reddy and Morris, for example, describe ToM as something that is now seen as "awesomely matter-of-fact—with a taken-for-grantedness hitherto reserved for those other staples of psychology such as 'growth spurt,' 'toilet training,' 'short term memory' and 'secure attachment'" (91). Williams, meanwhile, in looking at autobiographies written by high-functioning autistics, writes that "we do not usually have to *theorize* that other people have minds in order to understand and relate to them" (144).

explicit attributions and inference invitations to the narrator in the text, I believe that the reader will indeed mind read the narrator of a given text if they call attention to themselves, using the textual signals and features in order to create a continuing consciousness, as if they were another character. Theoretically, this may occur in any piece of literature, but in the case of some of Muñoz's narratives, mind reading the storyteller is perhaps more important than doing so for the characters, and is furthermore necessary in order to understand the underlying cultural schema of the stories themselves. As I mentioned previously, we notice Muñoz's vague narrator because of how they pull us into the text with carefully constructed narration gaps, but push us out when these gaps are never resolved.

MIND(ING) THE GAP

Iser would consider narration gaps as "indeterminate elements," components that serve to drive reader arousal in the text. In "The Reading Process," he explains that "if the reader were given the whole story, and there were nothing left for him to do, then his imagination would never enter the field [and] the result would be the boredom which inevitably arises when everything is laid out cut and dried before us" (51). Thus, as he explains in *The Act of Reading*, "what is concealed spurs the reader into action," and it is from this action that true reader-textual communication begins (169). In many cases, these gaps and blanks force the reader to "reconstitute" the text, a process of filling in gaps by evaluating what is both said and not said (169). For Iser, the reader is able to creatively fill in these gaps almost automatically through use of their imagination, and as Spolsky further explains, we do this because of innate cognitive structures engaged during the act of reading (2).

The narration gaps that I will consider in Muñoz's texts do indeed spur the reader into action—they are explicitly tied to plot development and need to be filled in order to fully understand the story. Just as is the case in most literature, these gaps are many times filled by the narrator, giving the reader a sense of closure. A clear example of this is found in "When You Come into Your Kingdom" from *Faith Healer*. Near the beginning of the story, we can infer from the tone of the narrator's description of protagonist Santiago that something is weighing heavily on him. After an exchange with a teenage coworker, the narrator writes that "the teenager's voice hangs with him—*I'm a junior in September*—the deep register, his Adam's apple knotty. He is a boy progressing solidly past adolescence, and Santiago thinks of his son Alejandro, but refuses the memory" (78). Here, the reader has direct insight into the mind of the protagonist—something is clearly bothering him—but we are also presented with a number of questions that serve to drive the momentum of the story forward. What is bothering Santiago? What does Alejandro have to do with Santiago's teenage coworker? Why does he refuse the memory? Eventually, we discover that a teenage Alejandro inadvertently committed suicide because his father constantly shamed him for being overweight, and he refuses the memory because it is still too painful.

This is exactly what the reader expects from most narrators—a guide through the story that presents narration gaps in order to pull us into the text, but also one that resolves our most critical questions by the conclusion. Nevertheless, in a number of Muñoz's stories, the narrator does not give us enough information to provide for closure, so we may need to go back to attempt to fill in these gaps, perhaps through a second reading, to create closure for ourselves. Here, we must also distinguish which sorts of narration gaps are likely to cause discord within the reader and which will not. In *What You See in the Dark*, the narrator does not reveal where Dan Watson flees to after the murder of girlfriend Teresa, although the text does hint around at various locations. Ultimately, I do not believe that this detail is important in the overall storyworld and thus does not count as a narration gap that may cause the reader to reexamine the text. Indeed, the reader may use their imagination to fill in these types of gaps, just as Iser envisions, but they are unlikely to make the reader stop and question the integrity of the text itself because it does not interfere with our overall understanding of the story.

Instead, when I talk of narration gaps in Muñoz, I refer to those that do inhibit our ability to understand the story—those that seem purposefully placed by the narrator in order to raise some sort of question within the reader in order to pull them into the story. What is salient in Muñoz's vague narrator is that they do not resolve the most critical gaps even though the answer may seem obvious to the reader, and it is this dissonance on the part of the narrator that pushes the reader out of the story in a search for closure. This narrator is employed in a number of Muñoz's stories, which may lead the reader to employ ToM to discern why the narrator is so coy with its audience, ultimately leading to the affirmation of the shared cultural schema of a shameful and hidden homosexuality.

"THEY DON'T NEED TO KNOW ANYTHING"

"Zigzagger," which opens the collection of the same name, immediately confronts the reader with several narration gaps that effectively set the tone for the rest of the book. Here, instead of focusing on what these gaps are, perhaps it is better to instead summarize what the narrator does reveal. The principal characters of the story are the boy, the father, and the mother, who are not given proper names. We know that the boy came home sick last night, vomited on the lawn, and his father and mother are now nursing him back to health. The mother is upset, while the father has become angry. The boy got sick after attending a dance, where it is implied that he consumed too much alcohol and attracted the attention of an older man. We also know that his friends come by to see him, but they insist that they do not know what happened to him at the party. The mother refuses to give them any information about his condition, insisting that "they don't need to know anything" (15). What may be immediately striking to the reader is that even though we do have a clear sense of who these people are and what their motivations may be, we are not given their names—instead, they simply go by the mother, the father, and the boy for the duration of the story. This may imply some sort of distance between the narrator and the characters, but this is contrasted with the fact that the reader is given personal insights into the various roles, particularly the mother. For example, as she is preparing a cream that she will use to heal the son (of what, we are not sure), the narrator writes:

> She is crying in the kitchen, mixing the mint and the oil and the water, and to make it froth, she adds a bit of milk and egg. The concoction doesn't seem right to her anymore, doesn't match what she recalls as a young girl, her grandmother taking down everyday bottles from cabinets and blessing their cuts and coughs. The mother does it without any knowledge, only guessing, but it makes her feel better despite feeling lost in her inability to remember. (9)

Here, the lack of names, implying a distance, is contrasted with the immediate closeness of knowing the personal thoughts of the mother and being able to pull from her memories and feelings with ease. This also occurs with the son, particularly when he is at the dance hall and catches the attention of the older man. Thus, we may also be led to believe that the narrator is purposefully obscuring their identities, but we are not told why.

In terms of plot, the critical narration gap of the story—what pulls the reader in—quickly becomes what happened to the boy. Given that the story is centered upon his illness and how distraught it has made his parents, the reader needs this critical piece of information in order to obtain narrative closure. As the story moves along, pieces of this gap are seemingly filled in by the narrator. The boy had a "violent sleep" as his parents watched over him through the night; his body "glistened, his legs kicking away the blankets as he moaned" (5). We know that the situation is severe because the mother has considered contacting a priest or a doctor, but the narrator also observes that they cannot call the former and have "him witness this" (8). There is also a "rotten smell" emanating from him (10), and the narrator makes sure to note that the mother is observing the boy closely, presumably in case his condition changes. However, these narrative pieces only lead to more questions, particularly when the mother is examining his legs. The narrator writes: "Her son's legs are hairless and cool to the touch. There are no raised veins. They are not reddened with welts. They are not laced with deep scratches made with terrible fingers" (10). Why would they be laced with deep scratches? Whose terrible fingers would have made the marks that do not exist?

Given that the narrator interlaces the home scene of the sick boy with the dance the night before, the reader is led to assume that something terrible happened at the event. The narrator tells that the boy attracted the attention of an older man at the dance, who the boy knew "was not like them" because he did not have an accent (14), and that they left together. With the question of what happened to the boy still in mind, the reader can assume that something will happen between him and the man. Somewhere outside, they have what might be able to be described as a sexual encounter, but again, the narrator does not make this clear:

> And though [the boy] felt he was in air, he saw a flash of the man's feet entrenched fast in the ground—long, hard hooves digging into the soil, the height of horses when they charge—it was then that the boy remembers seeing and feeling at the same time—the hooves, then a piercing in the depth of his belly that made his eyes flash a whole battalion of stars, shooting and brilliant, more and more of them, until he had no choice but to scream out. (17)

This passage is all that the story offers in terms of closure, but it is still fraught with ambiguities. On the surface, this may recount a sexual act, which would seem to connect with a fragment earlier that the boy had noted the man's handsomeness. There may also be indications that the man slipped the boy drugs when he offered the boy a beer (14), which may also explain why the boy was so sick when he arrived home. Nevertheless, the reader might also see this as the recounting of a beating of the boy by the man because of the former's sexual advances, particularly in how the boy recalls the man's feet with an animal-like comparison, then the piercing in his stomach, and his ultimate scream. This would also explain why the mother is preparing a cream, perhaps to rub on the boy's body to heal his wounds.

Here, we see a clear example of how the vague narrator carefully places these narration gaps, but when it comes to the critical pieces that would lead to understanding the entire story—what happened to the boy—the narrator becomes vague, pushing us out of the story in a search for closure. In essence, the narrator reveals everything, focalizing to an almost extreme extent at both the party and at home, but at the same time, reveals little to aid in our understanding of the plot. At this point the reader may mind read the narrator—why exactly does the storyteller refuse to clarify what happened to the boy? Does the narrator simply not know what happened? This seems unlikely given the details shared about the incident itself. A revelation about the mother may shed light on why the narrator takes this approach: "She believes, as she always has, that talking aloud brings moments to light" (18). If we are to believe that the man and the boy did have a sexual encounter, we can infer from this passage that homosexuality remains "hidden" if it is not talked about; thus, if the storyteller does not fill in all of the narration gaps surrounding the encounter, it does not become real. In Martínez's excellent reading of "Zigzagger," he calls this "shifting the site of queer enunciation" ("Shifting" 226). Even if the mother cannot speak aloud her son's homosexuality, she knows that it is present, and it is through her that the story communicates its effects.[7]

When I interviewed Muñoz, he explained that this story was about the boy's first sexual experience, one that he had with the devil. In that context, a number of elements from the story—the rotten smell, the idea of calling a priest—do make sense. While I did consider this during my original reading of the story, I also read it as the "boy" having such a terrible experience that the narrator metaphorically reconfigured the man as the devil. Nevertheless, Moya ties this story to the Mexican American folktale of "dancing with the devil," where a young woman pleads with her parents to go dancing, only to be wooed by a suave man who is, indeed, the devil ("Dancing" 251–52). In *The Social Imperative*, which I talked about at length

---

7. As Martínez writes, shifting recognizes that "queer experiences are actually *coproduced and shared* by larger collectives" (*On Making Sense* 16). He also observes this phenomenon in Muñoz's "The Unimportant Lila Parr" and "Good as Yesterday."

in the introduction, she further develops this into what she calls the vestigial schema—readers who share the cultural schema of the story of dancing with the devil will recognize it in Muñoz's story even though he does not explicitly mention it. Indeed, she believes that his telling of this folktale "can only be fully appreciated when it is placed in the context of the values, taboos, and symbolism of a larger Mexican American community" (100). This is an excellent example of the power of the cultural schema—being that I am not Mexican American, this story left me scratching my head in search of meaning, one that I ultimately placed in the idea of a shameful and hidden homosexuality because it fits within my own cultural schema as a gay male.

"HE STOPPED HIMSELF FROM COMPLETING THIS PICTURE"

"The Unimportant Lila Parr" is somewhat less vague than "Zigzagger" but delves into the same sort of cultural schema that we saw in that story. Here, the narrator introduces the reader to Lila Parr, a widower whose deceased husband gave their land to their neighbors, a husband and wife. These neighbors are the protagonists of the story, but just as in "Zigzagger," they are not given names, which may imply some sort of distance between the narrator and the story. Or perhaps the narrator does not reveal their names in order to strengthen the argument that they are not important—after all, if Lila Parr is "unimportant," how important could those who remain nameless be? The reader is quickly pulled into the story when the narrator observes that "he looks at his own wife, how she stands on the brink of something, and can see her anger begin to light from across the yard, how much she is beginning to resent being like Lila Parr, suddenly childless" (41). Suddenly, a narration gap is revealed—what happened to their child? If we are reading these stories in sequence, we may notice that this gap is similar to the one found in "Zigzagger," although here it appears that we will be given more information to provide for closure. Later, the narrator reveals further details when the couple identifies their son's body at the morgue:

> Their son's body was naked and discolored, his eyes closed.... The sheriff had told [the father] ... that their son may have been strangled, that two needles had been resting on the nightstand.... He knew that the culprit had been caught ... a young man the same age as their son. He knew that their son's body had been found naked and he stopped himself from completing the picture with that young man's involvement. (43)

It is clear that the father suspects that the son and the other "young man" were having some sort of sexual tryst, likely drug-fueled, but the narrator never completely writes those exact words in order to close this gap. What the narrator does relate are the insinuations of the townsfolk (43), and how rife with prostitution the motel is where the boy's body was found (45), implying that it is seedy. Again, as in "Zigzagger," the narrator comes close to closing the pivotal gap toward the end of the story, but again dances around the theme of homosexuality. The narrator writes, from the perspective of the motel owner:

> [The motel owner] has denied that the motel allows such illicit activities, that he has never found such things as needles or plastic bags. ... He will consider writing to the young man's father and explaining that it was all about love as well as anger.... He will write and tell him, plainly, that he saw the young man step out of the car. Then the other young man and how they stood by the door, close together and tentative, and then rushed inside. (46)

Nevertheless, this observation is nothing more than mere insinuation, just as with the townsfolk. That they stood "close together and tentative" does not necessarily imply that they were lovers, but this is the closest the narrator comes to filling in the main narration gap of the story—what happened to the son—which again pushes the reader out of the story in a search for closure. Read in conjunction with "Zigzagger," the reader again sees the cultural schema of hushed and shameful homosexuality—that, if it is not spoken aloud, it is less real.

The vague narrator appears a number of times in *Zigzagger*, including in the flash fiction story "Swallow." Here, the narrator immediately confronts the reader: "You were a boy then. You are a boy now" (47). The use of the second-person narration to open the story may disorient the reader, making it seem as though the narrator is addressing the audience directly. Fludernik writes that the effect of this is to play with the fact and fiction distinction in order to disorient, and in turn, reorient the reader (102). Of course, the reader of "Swallow" knows that they are not being addressed directly, but the use of this second person does force the reader to immediately take note of the narrator role. Although the story is just over a page long, the reader is presented with several narration gaps that they may attempt to resolve, pulling them into the story. After the first line, the narrator continues:

> Look at those boys. Those boys looking at boys. But this is about way back when, as a little boy, and how you mimicked. You mimicked in the backyard the things you saw. They took you to the circus and you saw the strong man. You eyed the strong man at the circus the way only a boy can. You admired him. (47)

Reading *Zigzagger* in sequence, the reader would likely realize that "those boys looking at boys" means that this is a queer-themed story—that the "you" referred to in the narration is homosexual. Iser speaks to this in theorizing that blanks and gaps force "combination" in search of meaning (Act 182)—thus, a reader may consider this story in the context of those that came before it in the collection in order to make meaning.[8] Nevertheless, if the story was not read in sequence, or perhaps taken out of the context of the larger collection, we may be able to consider the "you" more simply as boys who admire other males, perhaps as role models, something strengthened by the final line in this opening paragraph—"You admired

---

8. Iser further explains that blanks break up connectability in texts (*Act* 182), but I would instead argue that, at least in the *Zigzagger* collection, blanks actually work to force connectability and create meaning for the reader—in particular, the theme of a hidden and shameful homosexuality.

him." Notably, the narrator does not choose a more obvious phrasing, such "You were attracted to him," but rather something much more benign and playful.

As the story continues, this narrative gap is never fully resolved. In the last third of the story the narrator comes close, but again withholds, writing: "You know boys who've swallowed fire. They ache for fire. It sits in their bellies and burns. You'll burn too, your father tells you. You've burned already, for a strange boy who took you to a strange place. You did things that you no longer think are strange" (47–48). This passage could be interpreted in two different ways: first, as confirmation that "you" is indeed gay—strange things done with a strange boy—and the father is warning him that he will burn in hell for it. Alternatively, it could be seen as a much more care-infused warning from the father to be cautious when partaking in the dangerous, reckless things that young males sometimes do. Nevertheless, either of these readings still infuses reader-derived meaning that is not necessarily present within the story itself because the vague narrator does not fully resolve these narration gaps, pushing the reader out of the story in a search for closure. Again, as with "Zigzagger," the reader may ask why the narrator does not fully clarify the story, but in the case of "Swallow" that is a much more difficult question to answer given the short length of the story. Once again, the reader should perhaps take the advice of the mother in "Zigzagger": Some things are better left unsaid, and because homosexuality is not explicitly named, it is somehow less real for the narrator and "you" alike.

CRIMINAL LOVERS' QUARREL

This dance around the subject of homosexuality continues in "The Heart Finds Its Own Conclusion" from *Faith Healer*. Here, Sergio has landed in some sort of trouble, fleeing his home and urging his cousin Celia to pick him up at the bus station in Fresno. The immediate narration gaps presented to the reader are if Sergio will indeed arrive in Fresno, which worries Celia, and why he had to flee in the first place. Unfortunately for Sergio, his "trouble" has followed him by car, and arrives at the bus station in Fresno to confront Celia before Sergio arrives.

In this conversation, the reader may expect some of the narration gaps of the story to be easily resolved, but once again, the narrator remains elusive. After Celia asks the man what he wants from Sergio, he responds, "He's got my heart," which may push the reader toward the conclusion of a lover's quarrel. Nevertheless, the narrator immediately adds: "the man said, melodramatically, holding his hands across his chest, but he sneered a bit when he said it. 'He's got a lot of things I want back'" (58). The narrator's observations here are vague in themselves—a sort of confirmation of a lovers' quarrel, but in an ironic tone—and may not be enough to close this narration gap. Further along in the story, when Sergio finally arrives, the man violently reacts: "'You little fucker—you think I didn't know you'd come here?' The man hit Sergio hard against the back of his head, his palm flat and backed by the force of his rolling shoulders" (64). If this were a lovers' quarrel, one may expect a more melodramatic scene—could the situation possibly have a criminal element to it that the narrator does not reveal? The narrator never closes the gap, pushing the reader out of the story, so once again we may be led to consider the story as another in which homosexuality is spoken about in hushed tones, given the context of Muñoz's overall body of work.[9]

---

9. A younger Sergio appears in the story "The Comeuppance of Lupe Rivera," near the end of *Faith Healer*. Here, the reader receives confirmation of Sergio's homosexuality and learns that after a recent move from to Fresno from Bakersfield, "jilted boyfriends come . . . by the house and pound . . . on the door" (186). Thus, the reader can likely assume that the man in "The Heart Finds Its Own Conclusion" is also one of those "jilted boyfriends." The key difference between "Lupe Rivera" and "The Heart Finds Its Own Conclusion" is that the first is narrated by Sergio himself, who obviously has access to all the details of his own life, while the second is narrated in the third person, by a narrator who obviously does not have access to the same details. Muñoz frequently employs this strategy in *Faith Healer*—revisiting characters in later stories and picking up their thread from there. Overall, this strategy serves to create a more cohesive collection than his first, *Zigzagger*, although perhaps less interesting to look at from a narrative perspective.

Here, it could be argued that the vague narrator is instead merely unreliable, an area of narratology that has been studied extensively. However, I reject this—the narrator clearly knows what happened in these stories and does not try to confuse the reader, but instead leaves it up to them to put the pieces of the puzzle together.[10] Fur-

---

10. This idea of the unreliable narrator was first coined by Booth in his foundational 1961 work *The Rhetoric of Fiction*. He writes: "I have called a narrator reliable when he speaks for or acts in accordance with the norms of the work (which is to say the implied author's norms), unreliable when he does not" (158–59). Nevertheless, many critics have seen this definition as problematic given that it assumes that we can arrive at the heart of the implied author's "norms," when there is still much disagreement about what the implied author actually is. Chatman later theorized that the unreliable narrator may be employed to cast doubt on the "narrator's integrity, sanity, maturity, astuteness, sobriety, intelligence, or whatever" (*Reading* 242), while Nünning sees this role as manifesting itself in dramatic irony or discrepancy awareness. He further explains that "for the reader, either the internal lack of harmony between the statements of the narrator or contradictions between the narrator's perspective and his own concept of normality suggest that the narrator's reliability may be suspect" (58). Phelan sees six main types of unreliable narration, divided into two groups: misreading, misreporting, and misregarding, and underreporting, undereading, and underregarding (*Living* 51). He further explains that readers, upon encountering an unreliable narrator, must "reject those words, and, if possible, reconstruct a more satisfactory account; or . . . accept what the narrator says but then supplement the account" (50–51). It would be easy to categorize Muñoz's vague narrator as underreporting—purposefully telling less than they know (51)—forcing the reader to supplement with theories of their own. But we also must heed the distinction that Phelan makes between unreliable underreporting and reliable elliptical narration, specifically that the latter "leaves a gap that the narrator and the implied author expect their respective audiences to be able to fill" (52).

While I believe that we could consider some of Muñoz's stories as employing unreliable underreporting, particularly stories like "Campo" from *Zigzagger*, because homosexuality is such a recurrent theme in his works, narration gaps involving this theme become "fillable" very quickly; thus, considering this reliable elliptical narration rather than unreliable is much more plausible. I view Muñoz's use of the vague narrator as a precise artistic choice because of the anxieties it may produce in the reader—it forces them to pay attention to the text. Even if we consider the more classical view of the unreliable narrator as being in conflict with the norms of the implied author, here, the real author, Muñoz, is not in conflict with this entity, but rather uses it to construct a message in the text, and the reader will discover this as they move along in his collection to stories where homosexuality is an open topic.

thermore, not all of the queer themes in Muñoz's works are subject to narration gaps or shame. Indeed, many are quite open: In *Zigzagger*, "Good as Yesterday" tells of an openly gay teenager, a character that La Fountain-Stokes might call a proud sinvergüenza,[11] who falls in love with his sister's ex-boyfriend despite the consequences. "Skyshot" looks at a pair of lovers who are film buffs, and "By the Time You Get There, by the Time You Get Back" explores a father's relationship with his son and his son's unseen boyfriend. *Faith Healer* is full of tales of gay characters, including Sergio, whom we met earlier. If we read these stories in tandem, we will eventually be easily able to fill the narration gaps left by the vague narrator. Likewise, not all of the vague narration that Muñoz employs is exclusively found in queer-themed stories. In *Zigzagger*'s "Tiburón," kids anxiously await the man who sells shark teeth to come to town, and marvel at just how "valuable" these items are. Throughout the story, the reader may wait for some sort of indication as to what the significance of these teeth is, but none comes. Again, we have a narration gap that the storyteller does not fill in, but here it is much more difficult to mind read the narrator due to the lack of contextual clues in the story itself.

GAPS AS CULTURAL SCHEMA

Returning to the concept of the cultural schema, I believe that we may be able to consider Muñoz's works as exemplary in terms of how they approach homosexuality. This is strengthened by Phelan's idea of the layered ethical situation, of which he writes that "any character's action will typically have an ethical dimension and any narrator's treatment of the events will inevitably convey certain attitudes towards the subject matter and the audience" (Living 20). The cultural schema that we have seen so far in many of Muñoz's works

---

11. La Fountain-Stokes rejects what he sees as a call to embrace gay shame coming primarily from the white LGBT community, instead calling to Latinx *sinvergüencería*—"to be a sinvergüenza is to have no shame; to disobey, break the law, disrespect authority (the family, the church, the state), and in a perverse and curious way to be proud of one's transgression, or at the very least lack a feeling of guilt" (72).

is one of homosexuality being hidden and shameful, something also present in so many other gay Chicano narratives, including González's *Crossing Vines* and *Butterfly Boy*, Espinoza's *The Five Acts of Diego León*, as well as the novels of Arturo Islas, to name but a few. The way in which the vague narrator conveys the theme of homosexuality speaks further to the layered ethical situation, both in how the characters of a story such as "Zigzagger" cannot bring themselves to mention it and in how the narrator merely skirts the issue.

I also believe that the ordering of *Zigzagger* speaks to a further cultural schema as many of these vaguely narrated stories, where homosexuality represents a good deal of the narration gaps that the reader confronts, come in the first half of the collection. There are also a number of queer-themed stories in the second half of the collection, but the narration is not nearly as vague and the homosexuality of the characters is treated in a more open, honest manner. Some protagonists even find support in family members, such as Nicky, the gay teenager in "Good as Yesterday," and this trend continues in *Faith Healer*. I believe that Muñoz does this purposefully, perhaps to ease the reader into what is a heavily gay-themed collection, despite no outward indication of this on the book jacket or in reviews, and to further indicate a progression in how homosexuality has been viewed not only in the Chicanx community but also in the country at large.

CONFRONTING THE NARRATOR

To demonstrate the importance of story ordering, at the far end of the *Zigzagger* collection we come across the confrontational narrator, one who puts homosexuality directly in the face of the reader. This narrator is most prominent in "Monkey Sí," which tells the story of two young men from the Central Valley of California, Nestor and Tomás, who travel to San Francisco to visit a gay night club. Nestor is in love with Tomás, but it is not reciprocated because Nestor is not deemed as "acceptable" enough to date by the other. Their trip ends badly: When Tomás leaves the club for a tryst, Nestor is drugged and raped in an alley by two men who had been watching him closely.

When Tomás later returns to the club in search of Nestor, he eventually discovers that he has been taken to the hospital. The two flee the scene, scared of the hospital contacting their parents, and drive back to the Central Valley in almost complete silence. The narrator reveals that they never talk again—Tomás perhaps feels guilty and does not know how to approach Nestor, while Nestor seethes with anger because he believes that he would not have been raped had Tomás not abandoned him at the night club. Intensifying Nestor's anger is a surge of previously repressed feelings, specifically that Tomás never appreciated him at best, and was openly neglectful at worst.

Because of the emotive narration, it becomes very clear in the story who the reader is supposed to find sympathetic (Nestor) and who they are not (Tomás). Nestor is consistently drawn as a sympathetic, well-rounded, caring person, whereas Tomás is quite the opposite. Nestor dresses neatly (169), while Tomás does not (168); he is careful not to drink and drive even though Tomás insists that it "couldn't hurt" (171); and he buys Tomás's entrance into clubs while the latter "lingers by the doorman, as if forgetting that he has to pay" (171). The narrator goes as far as to interlace scenes of Nestor's rape with those of Tomás's tryst, writing that "Tomás is mean enough to wish that Nestor were there, watching this" (178), implying that he is downright cruel and vindictive, given Nestor's unreciprocated feelings.[12]

Although the narrator of the story is omniscient, privy to the thoughts of both Tomás and Nestor, he is also somewhat distant and removed from the text. At times it appears as though the narrator is describing a series of photographs or a television show and providing a running commentary. For example, the narrator writes:

> We can see then, from a distance, as a group of friends . . . but if we get close, if we let the adjectives take on their clothes (black pants,

---

12. This sympathy is also tinged with the aspect of race. Among the opening lines of the story, the narrator asks: "Do we already know that Nestor will lose out by the end of the story (and in life, because we have mentioned that he is dark skinned and small and these men don't like either)?" (167–68). This racial aspect is reinforced when the narrator writes that Tomás has given Nestor a number of nicknames, including "monkey" (177), hence the title of the story.

loose blue jeans, shiny shoes, shirts spread across impossible backs) . . . we would find that the group is a mangle of hesitations. We can see two of them trying to walk on either side of Tomás, that Nestor is alone and trying to keep up. (168–69)

There is almost a filmic quality to this vivid description, strengthened in the "close up" paragraph that immediately follows:

Later, if we like, we can get as close to Nestor as we want when we listen to Tomás tell him about why the two were walking on either side of him. Nestor will be on the telephone. . . . His heart will be beating fast and we will leave him alone to put down the receiver and do whatever he does when Tomás says these terrible things to him. (169)

At one point during Nestor's rape, the narrator asks the reader if we "want to see it happening? (We know what's happening)" (175). The narrator will describe this scene in great detail on the next page, but readers may be led to feel they can stop the story in its tracks, even though we know this is not possible unless we put the book down. The use of the "we" also serves to automatically include the reader in passing judgment on these characters, sharing in the narrator's thoughts and effectively pulling them into the story. "We" will leave Nestor alone "when Tomás says these terrible things to him" (169); "we" can consider Tomás insensitive "if we like" (174); "we" know that Tomás must resist internalizing the love that Nestor obviously shares for him (179); "we purse our lips at Tomás" when he does not look for Nestor before he leaves the club (175); and after Nestor is raped, "we will hate him as much as Nestor will for the rest of his life" (180). Our mind reading of the narrator tells us that he thinks Tomás is a bad person, and we, the reader, should think so as well.

But what if the reader does not agree with this assessment? Perhaps they may not blame Tomás for Nestor's rape, or they may have had a similar admirer that they had to shake off despite hurting their feelings. The judgmental narrator does open a space in the story for some sort of sympathy toward Tomás in spite of his overwhelmingly negative portrayal, perhaps so that those readers who side with him are not demonized as well. "We" know that Tomás thinks he has "bad blood," even if it doesn't mean much to "us" (173), and "if we follow Tomás, we will see him go home and lie in his bed, and he will cry" (181) after the trip to San Francisco, but ultimately, he does not know why he does this; "we can't know because Tomás doesn't have a clue, either" (181). At the same time, however, these descriptions almost serve to reinforce the negative judgment of Tomás given that he is incapable of rationalizing or explaining his emotions, even toward a sympathetic person such as Nestor. For those readers who still look past these details and take Tomás's side of the story, the narrator sets a trap near the conclusion, asking innocently: "Who do we care about? Who do we identify with?" (181). This allows the reader to perceive, perhaps, an opening for some sort of sympathy toward Tomás, or an "agree to disagree" split between those who sympathize with him and those who side with Nestor. But the narrator closes this door as quickly as it is opened. After describing Nestor sitting and eating cereal after the incident, he writes:

> His name is Nestor and some of us think he should levitate or endure something spiritual like that to close this story, floating right through the ceiling, sprouting wings. . . . Some of us will stay with him. Others of us won't (so go to Tomás, or Tommy, because he lets people call him that now). The rest of you can go to him on an invisible cloud. . . . We will stay with Nestor. (182)

Here, there is a clear split in the "we" narrator—those readers who may side with Nestor, whom we should side with according to the narrator, and the rest, the "you" who side with "Tommy," and it is those readers who are promptly pushed out of the story. In the end, the narrator is judging not only Tomás but also any readers who may side with his character. These readers, following the narrator's logic, should be ashamed of themselves for harboring such sympathies toward Tomás, and are effectively rejected from the story altogether. In summary, "Monkey Sí," even while still using the narrative push-pull that is a trademark of Muñoz, does not hide homosexuality from its readers—it confronts them with it, warts and all. Coming at the far end of *Zigzagger*, the reader who has made it this far needs no easing into the subject, so it is time to rip it wide open.[13]

CONCLUSION

This frank openness could very well turn off some readers, but that is the risk that comes with such narrative experimentation. Muñoz is difficult to define as a writer because his subject matter and approach to narrative vary so widely across the works he has produced so far. After publishing two more contemporary-set short story collections that feature a wide variety of queer characters, his subsequent *What You See in the Dark* was set in 1950s Bakersfield and centered on four females. In a narrative sense, it reaches back to *Zigzagger* in terms of experimentation, refusing to reveal who exactly is its second-person narrator until the last chapter of the novel. Again, this serves to pull the reader into the work—we want to know who this narrator is in order to put the various pieces of the puzzle together.

When looking at the confrontational narrator juxtaposed against the vague, we could say that the stronger that we are pulled into Muñoz's stories, the more forcefully we are pushed out. Given that the vague "Zigzagger" opens the entire collection, a reader may find it difficult to be pulled into the story because they have no frame of reference for Muñoz's writing, making it far easier to be pushed out, perhaps from the collection as a whole. This was my experience coming to his works through this collection—many of the stories are difficult to grasp because there is so much that the narrators do not tell. However, in a story such as "Monkey Sí," coming far later in the same collection, I would conversely propose that the reader is drawn far deeper into the story because the narrator is so completely abrasive, and we are consequently pushed out of the story far more strongly when it comes to the critical moment of siding with Nestor or Tomás.

---

13. In our interview, Muñoz recounted how he wrote this story in reaction to a rejection from a literary magazine because they did not publish "gay fiction." See chapter 5.

As previously mentioned, I believe that the vague narrator could also be considered an exemplary affirmation of a cultural schema, particularly if we read Muñoz's own words about being gay in a traditional Catholic family. In an interview with *Harvard Magazine,* he explained that "it's understood in my family that I am [gay], but we don't discuss it, which is a very typical Mexican Catholic response" (Porter Brown). This is perhaps indicative of how we can read the narrator in the stories highlighted earlier—it is understood that the characters in these stories are homosexual, but the narrator never quite arrives to the point of actually discussing it openly, instead talking around it, indicating some sort of shame regarding the topic. The first-person narrator of the story "Brother John" from *Faith Healer* also summarizes this sentiment: When Brother John is confessing a relationship he had with a man while he was away at school, the narrator, who does not share his own similar story, cuts him off rather abruptly. His reason is simple: "I learned a long time ago to keep things simple. Don't tell much. Don't tell everything. Don't reveal what people don't need or want to know. It makes it easier all around" (119).

CHAPTER 3

Unexpected Surprises and the Magic Realization of Espinoza's *Still Water Saints*

AS I MENTIONED in the introduction of this book, the three authors that I write about here have had vastly different publishing outcomes. Despite the breadth of his publication record, González has mostly published in smaller and university presses. This is not to diminish the importance of these presses solely because of their size—they have been critical in publishing many Latinx authors that may not have found space elsewhere. However, one of the disadvantages of being published in such houses is the smaller printing runs that they produce, and their limited ability to promote and place an author in the way that a larger firm such as Random House can. Indeed, some authors who start in these presses do jump to larger firms, like Muñoz, who moved from Northwestern University Press to Algonquin after his *Zigzagger* collection. It is far rarer for a first-time author to be picked up by a large firm, but this is exactly the experience of Espinoza, whose *Still Water Saints* was published by Random House in 2008. Landing at such a large firm is the dream of any novice author, but it also raises the question: How does a profligate author like González continue to go relatively unnoticed in the wider market, while newcomer Espinoza captures the attention of the largest publisher in the world?

In terms of the general field of Chicanx literature, this is one of the key questions that Martín-Rodríguez looks at in his foundational *Life in Search of Readers*. He believes that larger American publishers have effectively linked Latinx literature with magical realism and have worked to market this connection to the buying public, in large part because of the enormous influence that this genre has had on Latin American literature and its strong selling power (137). In this way, it stands to reason that these publishers are more likely to seek out works that have some sort of magical-realist bent to them, in order to fit within an already defined brand of what Latinx literature is, meaning less marketing and a greater potential audience who are accustomed to this connection. We see these dynamics at play in *Still Water Saints*—approaching the novel with little knowledge of the author, there is little reason to believe that it is *not* a magical realist work given that it seems molded to fit that genric schema, a concept explored in the introduction of this book. The cover and blurbs on the back of the book all strongly suggest that it fits this brand, and its first chapter, so important in setting the tone for the rest of the work, tells us that protagonist Perla "could walk on water," that she "summoned the spirits of the dead," and that "she fought the Devil"—all mystical elements. We will see further connections later in this chapter.

Although magical realism as a genre draws readers for a variety of reasons, it is also highly problematic for the literary critic and author.[1] With a primary formation in Latin American literature, I

---

1. In *Postethnic Narrative Criticism*, Aldama argues that critics too often view the use of magical realism as a "fusion of aesthetic and ethnographic artifact" (8). The author renames magical realism as "magicorealism" and examines the narrative as a storyworld in itself, instead of conflating it with the world outside of literature that the reader experiences (15–16). This chapter only considers magical realism as ethnographic fact insofar it applies to many Latinx authors who have been expected to produce these types of works. In terms of authors, Aldama argues that, as a matter of course, Latinx authors frequently choose between realist and magical-realist modes of storytelling, and that there is little difference between the two. As he explains in a later article, "they both reflect reality to the extent that by necessity their building blocks *are* building blocks taken from reality" (334), but magical-realist-based litera-

came to this chapter well aware of Mexico's *crack* manifesto, a literary movement that has attempted to break free of magical realism and chart a new course that would live up to the initial novelty of that generation of authors, whose membership includes legendary figures such as Gabriel García Márquez, Juan Rulfo, and Mario Vargas Llosa, among others.[2] The *crack* generation has rallied against clichéd magical-realist literature, holding up authors such as Isabel Allende and Laura Esquivel as "simplistic and formulaic" examples (Guerrero 5) that seem more intent on market success through capitalizing on a proven genre than producing any sort of literary novelty. Keeping in mind the idea of genric schema, I would consider all of these works, including those by Espinoza, Esquivel, Allende, and numerous other authors, to be magic *realized,* a term that encompasses many of the observations of Martín-Rodríguez that I will explore later. Instead of being a final product arrived at by chance, a magic-realized novel instead is produced through a series of practices informed by genric schema that serve to position a given work within the already established magical-realist genre, implying that this positioning is deliberate on the part of the publisher, and in some cases the authors themselves.

Nevertheless, just because a novel has been magic *realized,* it does not necessarily mean that it is magic *realist.* A curious thing hap-

---

ture also includes "events, actions, characterizations that do not conform to the laws of nature" (355). His explanation for how readers integrate this reality and unreality is something that I explore later in this chapter.

2. In "El *crack* en el vórtice de la novela mexicana," Eloy Urroz, one of the authors of the crack generation, explains: "Se creyó que atacábamos al realismo mágico y por ende a García Márquez, cuando sólo dijimos que nuestro desencanto era con algunas novelas epígonos del realismo mágico, las peores, las que no queríamos emular. Se creyó asimismo que renegábamos del boom o de la generación de Medio Siglo o de Contemporáneos, cuando se trataba justamente de lo contrario: de rendir tributo a estos tres grupos o momentos literarios con los que nos sentíamos y nos seguimos sintiendo deudores y herederos" (152) [It was believed that we were attacking magical realism and consequently García Márquez when we were just saying that we didn't like some of the inferior imitators of the genre, the worst ones, the ones that we didn't want to emulate. It was believed that we were renouncing the boom or the mid-century or contemporary generation when it was just the opposite: we wanted to pay tribute to these three groups and literary moments to whom we felt and still feel like both indebtors and inheritors].

pens as we advance through the pages of *Still Water Saints*: Despite all of its magic-realized rhetoric—the cover, blurbs, and opening chapter—virtually nothing occurs in the work that would fall outside of the empirical existence of the reader. Although protagonist Perla can walk on water and fights the devil, all of her "mystical" attempts at healing the customers who visit her botánica in Agua Mansa (a stand-in for Riverside, California) fail, sending her into a crisis of faith. There is nothing "magical" about this seemingly magical-realist work, which may be quite a surprise for the reader expecting such a reading experience, and I believe that this is where we find the true strength of the novel. This chapter will look at how Espinoza, through the use of cognitive surprise, not only effectively unwinds and discredits the idea that protagonist Perla possesses the ability to perform magic but also bends the borders of the apparent genre of the novel—magic realism—perhaps transforming the reader's genric schema of similar Latinx literature and uncovering important cultural schema at the site of the botánica itself.

Just as I looked González's use of affect in chapter 1 and theory of mind in Muñoz in chapter 2, here I will develop a cognitive theory of literary surprise in order to explore exactly how Espinoza upsets these readerly expectations. However, before entering into this discussion, I will further explore the idea of magic realization and genric schema, which will help us to understand why *Still Water Saints* appears to fit so neatly into this category. Given that one of the interests of this book is in exploring how Espinoza, González, and Muñoz each occupies a unique role in the emerging genre of gay Chicano literature, it is particularly important with *Still Water Saints* to look at how Random House and the author may have crafted this novel to fit within a genre that readers have come to expect from Latinx artists, even if the content of the work does not easily fit within its confines.

(MAGIC) REALIZING YOUR NOVEL

What is of particular interest in *Life in Search of Readers,* at least in the case of *Still Water Saints,* is Martín-Rodríguez's examination of the use (and abuse) of magical realism in the market (136), and how Chicanx (and Latinx works in general) have been typecast because of it. Given that magical realism has become almost synonymous with Latin American literature in the eyes of the American public, for better or for worse, market-directed Latinx literature has often been linked to it because it is a proven genre that has generated strong sales (137). Martín-Rodríguez reads this linkage as both a blessing and a curse: a blessing because it has helped to drive sales of Latinx works among a wider readership, and a curse because it has tropicalized this very same literature, effectively linking it with the Latin American literary tradition.[3] The effect of this is the negation of the very real history and novelty that Latinx literature has, presenting it as a foreign literature—something decidedly not American (126).

This magic realization of Latinx literature occurs in three ways, according to Martín-Rodríguez: on the covers of the books themselves, in the blurbs found on the back of the books and in other reviews, and in the production of new authors looking to be published. Because the author exerts most of their control over the content of the book (as opposed to the cover or blurbs), I will focus on that aspect in this chapter and set aside those other factors for chapter 4, where I will look at them in relation to all three of the authors in *Capturing Mariposas.* One of the worries of Martín-Rodríguez is that Chicanx authors are being conditioned to produce the types of works that retail sales indicate are in demand, even though it is the manipulation of the publishing houses that is distorting the market (128). Given that Espinoza was a new author at the time that *Still Water Saints* was released, how did he respond to this pressure? Given what we have already seen, it is plausible that Espinoza's creative writing process tilted toward magical realism if he desired to be

---

3. As Robbins explains, a similar process has also occurred with Latin American literature chosen for publication in Spain. In "Globalization, Publishing and the Marketing of Hispanic Identities," the author explains how Alfaguara, a Spanish publisher, has numerous branch offices in Latin America that both sell to the local market and choose books to sell in Spain, a more lucrative market. Those works that make the voyage across the Atlantic, she explains, tend to represent Latin America as feminine, indigenous, and, above all, exotic (99).

published in a major venue, and the fact that the novel was picked up by Random House might suggest that he did follow this path, either subconsciously or by choice.[4] As we will see in chapter 4, the cover and blurb reviews all would seem to indicate that *Still Water Saints* is a magical-realist novel, but there are also a number of elements within the book itself that work to strengthen this assumption.

The novel contains eight chapters, each of which is divided into two parts. Generally, the first section tells some sort of story about Perla and her botánica, while the second is about a member of the community who either purchases something from the store or enters by happenstance. The only chapter that does not follow this model is the very last one, for reasons that will be touched upon later. *Still Water Saints* follows a year in the life of Agua Mansa, California, and as an extension of this, chapters are titled by month and day, organized around a particular saintly feast. For example, the first chapter is "January 6: Feast of the Epiphany of Our Lord & Día de los Reyes," while the last is "December 12: Feast of Nuestra Señora de Guadalupe." While the attributes of these saints are most times only loosely connected to the content of the particular chapter, for a potential reader browsing the book, this structure may appear to fit the magical-realist "brand," which, for our purposes here, is synonymous with the idea of genric schema. It may even be reminiscent of the structure of Mexican author Laura Esquivel's 1989 debut novel, *Como agua para chocolate,* a popular magical-realist work that was later made into a well-received movie. Esquivel's novel contains twelve chapters, one for each month of the year, all beginning with a particular recipe. While the theme of food is not used in *Still Water*

---

4. In "Postmodern Continuum," McCracken explores how Latina authors, specifically those of high art and "chica lit," negotiate market demands. She writes that "while writers such as Julia Alvarez, Ana Castillo, Cristina García, and Denise Chávez negotiate and sometimes internalize the demands of mainstream publishers as they attempt to write works of art, chica lit writers such as [Alisa] Valdes-Rodriguez, Mary Castillo, Caridad Piñeiro, and Michele Serros aim for the widest audience possible and follow formulas for commercial success" (166). I believe that *Still Water Saints* falls somewhere in between these two realities—to a certain point, Espinoza does follow the commercially successful magical-realist brand, but he also subverts it to a significant extent, as we will see later.

Saints, each chapter is labeled as the "Feast" of a particular saint, which strengthens the comparison.

Aside from the structure of the novel, the theme of religion and the mystical prevalent on the cover and in the chapter titles themselves is another feature that fits the "brand" of a good deal of Latinx (and indeed Latin American) magical-realist literature. If the reader has read reviews beforehand, they will know that the novel centers upon Perla, a curandera, similar to Rudolfo Anaya's *Bless Me, Ultima,* one of the most well-known Latinx works published. Taking this further, from the very first page of the novel, Espinoza establishes the idea that Perla is indeed special by instilling her with supernatural powers. In the opening lines of the novel, he writes:

> She could walk on water.
>
> She roamed the banks of the Santa Ana, among the long green stalks, chanting to the moon, to the gods of Night and Shadow. She rose and stepped onto the river, her footsteps gently rippling the surface. (3)

As the chapter progresses, Espinoza works to further strengthen this connection: "She summoned the spirits of the dead," "She fought the devil. Every night he came to her," and finally, a few lines later, "She was a bruja. A Santa. A Divina. A Medium, Prophet, and Healer" (3). After several vignettes of a number of the customers who have come into the store seeking help, Espinoza closes the chapter in Perla's house, describing how an opossum outside of her house becomes a sign that trouble is brewing. He writes: "She took another drink and closed her eyes. That animal. It was a messenger. It was letting her know. Something was out there. It was coming. She sat down and waited for it" (13). Aesthetically, a reader in search of the magical-realist "brand" would certainly be led to believe that they had found it in *Still Water Saints*—the cover and title both suggest magical/mystical elements, the reviews refer to how "bewitching" the novel is, and the first chapter asserts that protagonist Perla fights the devil and walks on water. *Still Water Saints* appears to have it all, at least at first glance. As Bauman explains, this is the seduction of capitalism: "[the] straightforward sensual job of tasty eating, pleasant smelling, soothing or enticing drinking, relaxing driving, or the joy of being surrounded with small, glittering, eye-caressing objects" (50–51). Nevertheless, the rest of the novel is not so enticing for those readers who are expecting magic to happen, a subversion of expectation that I believe Espinoza accomplishes using the element of literary surprise.

There has been surprisingly little work done with surprise in literature, unlike the substantial fields that support both theory of mind and sympathy/empathy that we saw in the previous chapters. Perhaps this lack of attention is because surprise is so common—while the average person is likely unaware of ToM, even if they do use it in their everyday lives, and perhaps cannot articulate the difference between sympathy and empathy, surprise is something that we feel we can easily explain because it is so often experienced. As Meyer, Niepel, et al. write, it was conceived as an original emotion by Descartes in 1649, while others see it as a primary or fundamental feeling (296), making it, arguably, as easy to explain as the concept of happiness or sadness. The concept of surprise may seem rather simple, and although it has not yet been substantially employed in literary studies, there is an extensive amount of cognitive science that has looked into how people experience and process different types of surprise.[5] Here I will review some of this literature, and then move toward a theory of surprise in literature and finally to how Espinoza uses it to challenge the expectations of his readers.[6]

---

5. A number of studies in surprise also come from the field of artificial intelligence, wherein one of the primary concerns is modeling for unexpected events. Computers have been good at predicting and handling the predictable, but they may fail when presented with something they were not expecting. Ortony and Partridge, for example, cite a hypothetical drink-preparation robot that may not know how to process a glass that has been glued to the cupboard because such a highly unlikely—surprising—event has not been modeled (108).

6. Although I will not enter into studies done with fMRIs, as is now more common with cognitive-based studies, there does exist a neural basis for surprise. Michelon et al., for example, look at the neural correlates for incongruous visual information, for example, showing subjects a series of normal pictures and then, suddenly, one in which the head of a wrench has been fused onto a sheep's body (1612). What the authors find is that "signal increases were greater for incongruous versus ordinary and oddball stimuli throughout the

SURPRISE UNDER THE MICROSCOPE

As a base to this discussion, I turn to Meyer, Niepel, et al., whose 1991 study "An Experimental Analysis of Surprise" is often cited by other scholars in the field. As these authors explain, "surprise is assumed to interrupt other ongoing processes, to direct attention to the surprising stimulus, and thus to enable the organism to respond adaptively to sudden changes in its environment" (296). For these authors, surprise "restructures" the schema of the person being surprised—what they are expecting based on previous experience—and results in the following processes:

> (a) to anticipate and control future occurrences of the previously discrepant event (i.e. to bring it about or to prevent it); (b) to avoid the event if it turns out to be negative and uncontrollable; or (c) to ignore the event if it proves to be irrelevant with respect to further action.[7] (297)

In their later article, Meyer, Reisenzein, and Schützwohl tread similar ground, but limit their study to one particular aspect of surprise: the action-relevance check, or how pertinent the surprise is in relation to schema of ongoing events (251). They define schema as "informal, unarticulated theories about objects, situations, and events. To fulfill their functions, these informal theories must be at

---

ventral and dorsal visual pathways, and in prefrontal cortex bilaterally. Signal decreases were larger for incongruous than for ordinary stimuli bilaterally in lateral parietal regions. A subset of regions near the right frontal operculum and extending laterally responded only to, or more strongly to, infrequent incongruous pictures." In addition, incongruous images were recalled better than congruous ones (1612). What this seems to suggest, aside from there merely being a neural basis for surprise, is that surprising events may be remembered better than ordinary sequences. This is also suggested in non-fMRI empirical data presented by Iran-Nejad, which will be explored later in this chapter.

7. The details of the author's particular experiment are not entirely relevant, but in general, they aim to discover how much being surprised delays the interrupted action being performed and how much involuntary attention is given to the interrupter, and to measure the "subjective experience of surprise" on the part of the participants of the study (297).

least approximately correct, which in turn requires that they are continuously monitored" (253). This implies that schema is an expectation of a certain state or behavior, even if that behavior is unspoken. For example, because Bill knows, even if subconsciously, that Mary always stops by his office around 10 a.m., this event becomes part of his background schema. If Mary does not stop by his office at 10 a.m. one day, Bill would be surprised because it disrupts his schema. In summary, these two fundamental studies both appear to treat surprise as some form of expectation failure.

Reisenzein would later add another aspect to this, proposing that there is a "cognition of unexpectedness produced by the schema-discrepancy check" (267), wherein "the appraisal of unexpectedness involves a special-purpose, hardwired mechanism that outputs a nonpropositional signal whose intensity reflected the degree of schema-discrepancy" (267). To use our example above, Mary not stopping by Bill's office on a particular day may not send a strong signal of surprise to Bill, but Mary stopping by, her face bloodied, likely would. For Reisenzein, this makes surprise inherently subjective—what is surprising to some may not be to others, and what encodes a distinct event as surprising is unique to the developed schema of each person within the context of particular situations.

Ortony and Partridge, however, believe that there is much more to surprise than just expectation failure (106). These authors see surprise as stemming from two distinct types of input: the deducible, more in line with expectation failure, and the nondeducible, which is where we encounter true surprise. For example, one craving escargot may go to a French restaurant, but if the establishment does not sell this item, it would properly be called expectation failure because this rule—that a French restaurant typically sells escargot—is usually true (an active expectation), but not always (107). On the other hand, if a rock comes "hurtling through one's window in five minutes" (106), this could properly be labeled surprise because there is no reasonable expectation of that occurring—it is completely nondeducible. Other times, surprise occurs when beliefs are immutable. To use the above example, there is no reason to believe that a French restaurant will serve anything but French food; thus, entering such an establishment and being given a menu solely composed of Greek entrées violates this immutable belief, and therefore is a surprising event (107). As the authors explain, true surprise is typically nondeducible and may even be startling, whereas expectation failure rarely is, or falls very low on such a scale (108).[8]

Lorini and Castelfranchi sum up the body of research on surprise by constructing two basic models: mismatch-based surprise and astonishment, both of which would seem to track Ortony and Partridge's model of the deducible and the nondeducible. For Lorini and Castelfranchi, mismatch-based surprise is explained as "actively checking whether a certain event is happening," having an expectation of the next input, and then "attempt[ing] to match the incoming data against it. If there is a mismatch (conflict) between the two representations there is surprise" (3). The authors further explain that "the intensity of this form of surprise is a function of the probability assigned to the expectation conflicting with the perceived fact" (3). Astonishment, meanwhile, is found in perceiving a fact, and then recognizing the sheer implausibility of it, necessarily meaning that it could not be predicted (3). These authors also believe that there must be a more careful distinction between types of surprise, particularly in terms of degree. The primary difference between mismatch-based surprise and astonishment, they assert, appears to be in the degree of difficulty in assimilating the surprise occurring in the latter (11). As they explain, "generally in order to cope with an intense astonishment, I need a deep and large revision of my well consolidated beliefs," which may not be the case in mismatch-based surprise (11). Lorini and Castelfranchi also make the case that belief change stemming from surprise, something also theorized by others such as Meyer, Niepal et al., and Meyer, Reisenzein et al., "is only triggered under certain specific preconditions" (24). The higher the level of surprise, they explain, the "higher the probability that the agent will revise its knowledge" (25). I will return to the idea of belief change, and specifically its potential application to literature, later in this chapter.

---

8. The authors do provide such a scale. See 107.

THEORIZING SURPRISE IN LITERATURE

Although there is a relative paucity of studies of literary surprise, one of most often cited articles in this area is Kintsch's "Learning from Text." This author proposes that "how much one knows, what expectations are generated during reading, and how a text can be organized in a coherent manner" (91) all form the basis of reader interest, and all "point to the importance of the reader's knowledge structure in the comprehension process" (91). Kintsch calls what the reader already knows the "apperceptive mass"—we could also consider this to be schema—and he further explains that "relatively small deviations from expectations, misfits between the apperceptive mass and new information are interesting and provide the right conditions for learning, which is now conceived of as a correction or addition to existing knowledge structures" (93). Furthermore, although the reader should not be able to routinely predict what they are about to read, they should be able *postdict* it, meaning that it should make sense in retrospect. In terms of literature, Kintsch believes that the author must be capable of surprising the reader by providing unexpected turns in the narrative, but when the entirety of the story is read, it should form an "integrated whole" (97). If it does not "negate the knowledge structure that the reader has already formed" within the context of the narrative, it will likely be perceived as interesting (97). Thus, in Kintsch's case, surprise in literature is ultimately linked to the work's ability to entertain the reader.

Brewer and Lichtenstein follow this theory in their development of the oft-cited structural-affect theory of stories, which establishes a basic set of guidelines that predict the amount of entertainment a hypothetical reader would derive from a narrative. They explain that story schema can be generally reduced to the use of surprise, suspense, and curiosity, and that entertainment is derived from a combination of these elements. In terms of surprise, they explain:

> A surprise event structure must contain critical expository or event information early in the event sequence. In a surprise discourse

organization, the critical information from the beginning of the event structure is omitted from the discourse, without letting the reader know that it has been omitted, and then is inserted later in the discourse. We assume that the reader will be surprised when the reader reaches the point where the omitted information is revealed, and that the surprise is resolved when the reader reinterprets the underlying event sequence in light of this new information.[9] (480)

Other researchers have sought to put this structural-affect theory to empirical testing. Hoeken and von Vliet, for example, discovered that a story that evoked surprise also resulted in a higher level of overall appreciation of the story (285), and readers were better at answering questions afterward, suggesting that surprising elements force readers to pay more attention (286).

Iran-Nejad, meanwhile, has looked at the causes of interest and liking in literature, with a particular focus on what effect surprise exerts on audience reception. The author discovered that readers found themselves interested in stories that have resolved endings, both in the case of works with medium- or high-level surprises (128). She also found that readers are not interested in surprise for the sake of surprise—those stories with surprising endings that did not "resolve postsurprise incongruity" were rated lower, supporting the claim that "surprise per se does not create interest" (128). The author also found that surprise had no effect on whether or not a reader liked a story (128), which may imply that ultimate reader "liking" judgments may be more based on content, style, writing, or characters rather than plot structure alone.

The studies that I have looked at here are more classically narratological in nature, even if some have used empirical data. Unfortunately, there are few that look at surprise with the much more recent scientific-cognitive turn of mind. One that is of interest in this chapter is Tobin's "Cognitive Bias and the Poetics of Surprise," which

---

9. Here, we also see a clear opening for Muñoz's narration gaps, although I would not classify his narrations as particularly surprising given that, many times, we must self-fill these gaps.

turns to theory of mind to explain why and how we may enjoy some types of literature. Tobin asserts that stories that aim to entertain should be surprising (157), and, using the particular example of mystery novels, the critic explains that readers tend to enjoy more well-constructed works that perform a "narrative rug-pull" (157). She says that this happens when a work presents facts in a way to make the reader believe something to be true, only to change this "truth" later in the novel. In order for this to work, she explains that clues must be laid out throughout the work that point to the ultimate truth, but done in a way that we may overlook them, which we do because we readers tend to "align our perspectives by default with perspectives presented in a discourse" (165).

Tobin uses theory of mind to explain how readers may feel that they know what a particular character is thinking, and explains that the surprising element may be that the character is thinking something entirely different. I do believe that there is a space here for the clinical studies of surprise reviewed above, particularly in that there is a mismatch between what we believe will happen and what actually occurs. When this narrative "rug-pull" occurs, the reader then goes back and reevaluates their beliefs to decide if this turn of events is narrative "fair play," as Tobin puts it (157), or instead comes out of nowhere, which may lead the reader to discount the logic of the book as a whole. Although the author does not use Kintsch's term "postdictability," it seems to closely encapsulate what she describes. Although I exclusively discuss literature here, the idea of fair play is applicable to any sort of narrative. A good recent example would be the final season of the television drama *Lost*, which effectively pulled the narrative rug out from under the viewers in the series finale. This led some viewers to go back and reevaluate the series in light of new information, while others judged it as narrative sleight-of-hand and dismissed the show as a whole.[10]

---

10. Even years after the series ended, this debate still rages on, as a visit to any number of internet message boards will attest to. It seems that for those who believe that *Lost* was primarily a character-driven drama, satisfaction with the series finale is high, while those who saw the series as science fiction were left cold.

This discussion of surprise also has strong consequences for the idea of the generic schema, which I have referenced throughout this book. For the average reader not well versed in the academic discussion of what constitutes particular genres, their conceptualization would typically come from firsthand experience of what they have already consumed, or what they have been conditioned to expect. In short, they likely form their own generic schemas that act as a guide when browsing and reading literature, a process highly informed by marketing done by publishing houses. Using the example of *Still Water Saints*, when a reader sees the title, looks at the cover, and/or reads the reviews, these things may recall other magical-realist works or indeed other Latinx works that have likewise been magic realized in the way that Martín-Rodríguez describes, thus setting up certain readerly expectations before they turn the first page.[11] Recalling Kintsch, we may be able to consider the generic schema as part of the reader's apperceptive mass—the sum of what they already know about magical-realist literature.

It could be argued that surprise would be generated within the discourse of magical-realist fiction (or, by extension, any other genre of work) when events occur that go against the schema of what the reader knows to be logical and rational in their everyday life. For example, in Isabel Allende's first novel, *Casa de los espíritus,* there is a well-known passage in which Marcos, an uncle of the protagonist, builds a "flying machine" out of crates, then takes off and disappears over the mountain range. This could be considered surprising for a reader given that it would generate a mismatch against the schema of what we know to be physically possible: We would expect his flying machine to crash shortly after takeoff, or not lift off the ground at

---

11. Kagan also uses a schema of semantics in his study *Surprise, Uncertainty and Mental Structures*. The author asserts that the formation of a class schema depends upon the "essentialness" of a feature, how often it is experienced, the context, and the significance (43). For the reader who seeks out magical-realist works, it could be assumed that they have already developed a particular schema for this type of work given the reinforcement of this genre via various methods by authors and publishers, as already discussed. For readers new to this area, I believe that the magic realization of *Still Water Saints* is strong enough to form a new schema that they may later apply to other works.

all because it is impossible to build an airplane out of crates. Nevertheless, I would argue that this event is only superficially surprising because it is something that the reader would expect from a novel that employs magical realism. In short, when a reader picks up this type of novel, there is an unspoken contract that they will suspend their disbelief and accept as possible whatever happens in the novel.

As Aldama explains, the idea of gap-filling, which we saw as critical in Muñoz's texts, also plays a key role here. When we are aware that we are reading a magical-realist narrative, "we gap-fill the same way as we would with a realist text, it's just that the blueprint guides us to gap-fill without further ado and no explanation is given regarding events, actions, or characters that do not conform to the natural laws that govern our everyday experiences" ("Magical" 337). I would push this assertion further—the reader may highly anticipate events and characters that do not conform to the laws of nature, and become disappointed when these narrative pieces do not act as we anticipate. Here, I can cite my own example of reading Anaya's *Bless Me, Ultima*—aside from enjoying the content of the novel itself, I read in anticipation of the curandera Ultima doing something magical or curandera-*like*, at least according to my schema of what a curandera is and does.

In other forms of media, we could consider one of American television's longest running dramas, *Law & Order*. Any viewer knows that at some point in the episode, there will be a narrative rug-pull that fingers the true culprit of the crime in question, typically a character that the viewer had already became acquainted with but dismissed as culpable of the crime for some reason or another. To return to Lorini and Castelfranchi, is the viewer experiencing mismatch- based surprise or astonishment in this example? I would say that both are possible, but with the caveat that we fully expect this surprise to come and eagerly await it—it is *predictably* surprising. Thus, it could be said that we derive enjoyment from watching *Law & Order* largely from the expected narrative surprise and the buildup to it, just as readers who consume magical-realist fiction may derive pleasure from events that fall outside of their realm of experience—they are predictably surprising. To summarize Bauman, for the audience, these expected surprises become our narrative "tasty eating."

In order to examine the impact of distinct varieties of surprise in literature, or any sort of medium that plays in well-known genres, I would instead speak of the *expected* surprise, and, on the other side, the *unexpected* surprise. Cognitively, an expected surprise is anticipated because the work, in its structure or form, recalls some sort of schema from our memories that the narrative fits into. The unexpected surprise, meanwhile, comes unanticipated because it goes against the schema that we have assigned to a given piece of literature, or whatever we are consuming. For example, the *Law & Order* investigators finally figuring out who really committed the crime is a predictable surprise, whereas a nuclear bomb suddenly detonating over New York City halfway through the episode would be completely unexpected because the viewer's schema of this series is that of a crime-procedural drama, not science fiction. This event would also be quite astonishing for the viewer, not a mere mismatch with what they were expecting, and may indeed have the power to alter the genre categorization of a work *if* the audience is able to accept such a narrative rug-pull.

To integrate this with earlier literature referenced above, I believe that we may find both mismatch and astonishment in either type of surprise,[12] but also that these types of surprises have more far-reach-

---

12. It would seem that in a given genre that relies upon the "expected surprise," the idea of surprise is rather moot because the reader knows that something of this nature will happen. In these cases, I believe that mismatch or astonishment occurs not by the mere existence of the surprise, but rather because of its content. Tobin outlines this idea in "Cognitive Bias," where she seems to write primarily of mismatch-based surprise, which may mean that the character that we are led to believe committed a crime is actually innocent. This is mismatch-based surprise because as we read, we form our own theories, even subconsciously, that may or may not be what is eventually revealed. I would further theorize that astonishment-based surprise is much more difficult to achieve in literature, or in entertainment in general, because it must come from the proverbial left field but still adhere to the internal logic that the work has established. A good example of astonishment would be the murder of protagonist Marion Crane (Janet Leigh) in the movie *Psycho*. Leigh was among the top-billed actors in the movie, so her character's murder less than halfway into the picture was a shock for audiences. Coming from director Alfred Hitchcock, audiences would certainly have *expected* a surprise to occur, but the murder of the protagonist, accompanied by graphic detail highly unusual for the era, could accurately be described as astonishing.

ing consequences when they are unexpected simply because in order to understand/interpret them, we must not only change the schema that we have developed for the given work but must also fight against our genric schema as a whole.[13]

The use of the unexpected surprise is also how I consider Espinoza to bend the borders of magical realism in *Still Water Saints*, especially for those readers who come to the novel expecting a certain type of literary experience. Here I could exclude hypothetical readers who are new to the magical-realist genre, or who have no expectations whatsoever of Latinx literature. Nevertheless, I do believe that they would react with the same sort of surprise to *Still Water Saints* as an informed reader due to the idea of the mystical that is emphasized on the cover, the blurbs on the back of the book, and reviews. In the case of these readers, the first chapter of the novel becomes even more important—Espinoza makes it clear that Perla has magical powers. Thus, while reading, the uninformed reader may form an active schema as to what they are expecting from the rest of the novel, one that will be necessarily altered as they continue reading the work. In short, Espinoza's novel may create an entirely new genric schema of Latinx literature in this particular type of reader.

STILL WATER SAINTS' UNEXPECTED SURPRISES

As we have seen, for a potential reader considering purchasing Espinoza's novel, it would likely activate the genric schema associated with magical realism, or perhaps schema of mysticism or the occult

---

13. As I will explore later in the case of *Still Water Saints*, Lorini and Castelfranchi believe that the stronger the surprise is, the more likely that it will result in belief change. Thus, we may be able to consider any type of astonishment provoked in the audience as a strong indicator of belief change, whether it stems from an expected or an unexpected surprise. This would be like the case of the murder of Marion Crane in *Psycho*, which, as an event, added a new dimension to what horror movies could do to their protagonists. This is something that filmgoers would likely take into account for future such films, resulting in belief change.

if the reader is not familiar with these works. Given this, the reader would likely anticipate a number of "expected surprises" from the novel—perhaps magic, as the author alludes to in the opening, or other events that fall outside of the realm of common experience. Nevertheless, instead of offering these expected surprises, I believe that Espinoza delivers a series of unexpected surprises in the novel, ultimately unraveling the idea of magic and the idea that the protagonist Perla actually possesses some sort of otherworldly power. Here, I will look at how Espinoza accomplishes this throughout the series of interconnected stories that form the novel, then later explore how he bends the borders of the genre itself.

After the first chapter characterizes Perla as a curandera who is able to perform a number of otherworldly acts, the subsequent chapter quickly works to put this ability into doubt. Here the reader is introduced to Rosa, a teenager who has gained a significant amount of weight. Her mother has purchased a special tea from Perla's botánica to help her shed this heft, but Rosa's sister, Blanca, is rather skeptical, even though their mother asserts that the tea is working because Rosa has already lost five pounds (14). What the reader might expect at this point, given what the novel has just told us about Perla's abilities, is for Rosa to continue losing weight, validating Perla and her remedies. Nevertheless, this is not what happens—Rosa herself lays doubt onto Perla because her weight has fluctuated even while drinking the tea, and she believes that her weight loss may be more attributable to increased exercise than anything else. Even Perla encourages her to continue exercising—to "do everything you can to keep the weight off"—but Rosa ends up rejecting her and the tea, leaving the store (28). Perla insists that she will wait until Rosa is "ready" to return (28), but she never does, and she is supported in this decision by her new boyfriend, who also doubts Perla's powers. While this may seem a rather small piece of unraveling Perla's mysticism, it is significant because it occurs immediately after she is built up as a woman who fights the devil and walks on water, but here she cannot perform a much simpler task—helping an overweight teenager lose weight.

Through the eyes of transvestite Azúcar, the chapter "Así Like Magic" portrays Perla as fumbling for answers to what should be simple questions given her supposed prowess. Azúcar has stopped by the botánica to buy a candle to light for a friend who recently died, and also picks up a rosary. Azúcar notes that she has never really believed in such things and does not know how to pray a rosary (96), so she asks Perla what will happen if she does not pray it in time. Perla's response, instead of coming from a place of decades of experience with mystical powers, is rather uncertain and rambling: "After that it's too late," she says. "They stay stuck in Purgatory. Or here. Ghosts haunting houses and cemeteries. Not good for them. Not good at all" (95). Here, the reader may attempt to mind read Perla because it is rather easy to see through her answer to the question. Although we do not have textual insight into her physical reaction, we can almost picture her eyes becoming wide as she stumbles through the consequences of the delayed prayers, hoping that Azúcar does not question her any further on the subject and fails to notice that she clearly does not know what she is talking about.

A more confident Perla returns in "Aftershocks," when Nancy, who has just returned to Agua Mansa, goes to Perla to buy a remedy to help her ailing father. In this case, the negation of Perla's powers takes place much later in the novel, when, in the final chapter, Nancy returns to the botánica and reveals that her father has since slipped into a coma (234). We see a confident Perla once again in "Taking Stock," when Shawn buys a candle from her in order to drive his roommate's girlfriend away. He carefully follows her instructions to "carve the name of the person [he is] trying to get rid of into the top of the candle" and tie a piece of cloth belonging to the girlfriend around it while it burns (153). The reader never discovers if the candle works or not, but Shawn does lose his job at the end of the chapter because of a scam he was running, implying that he is visited by some sort of karmic justice despite Perla's "help."

In the final example that I will use, the reader may be surprised to learn that Perla is not viewed as a sage by everybody in the community, but instead is seen by some as just an annoying old woman. In "Braceras," Perla hires Lluvia to paint a mural of the Virgin of Guadalupe on the side of her building, but instead of appreciating the knowledge and encouragement that Perla shares, Lluvia considers her a bothersome busybody. In the following passage, the reader may once again employ theory of mind to read Lluvia, whose curt, snide answers give away her mental state. As Perla settles in to watch Lluvia paint, she says:

> "I have to be careful," she says, adjusting herself in her chair, draping a towel over her shoulders. . . . "Don't you get scared? Working out in the sun?"
>
> "No."
>
> She calls me hija and says she has an oil inside the shop. "It doesn't have sunscreen, hija. But it can give you some protection."
>
> "I'm cool," I say. "Look." I hold both arms out. "See? No cancer here."
>
> "Huh. Not yet. Then ten years from now you get this spot and next thing you know it's all over." (224–25)

Although Lluvia does appear to come to appreciate Perla by the end of the chapter, it is clear that she initially sees her as an elderly woman with too much time on her hands, not a figure worthy of reverence for her sage advice and mystical powers. In their sum, this series of unexpected surprises slowly unravels the apparent magic of Perla by mismatching our schema of what she should be, and how other characters should treat her, given the magic realization of the novel itself.

In this context, the most important unexpected surprises for the reader may be found in the saint-themed companion chapters, where we learn more about Perla's life and her path to becoming a curandera. In "The Feast of San Gabriel the Archangel," the reader learns that she did not come to "walk on water" because of some divine calling, but rather because she was rebelling against her husband, Guillermo. On a slow, rainy day at the store, she confesses in writing:

> I am ashamed of the fact that I only agreed to do this job because it would get me out of the house. Guillermo spent all those years working, leaving me alone in the afternoons. No kids. No nothing. I felt like I had no life. Like things could have turned out differently if I'd only married someone who could give me more. (67–68)

In this chapter, the reader is also given more background on the man who first opened the botánica, Señor Darío, initially believed by the people of the neighborhood to be the devil because of the things he advertised, such as tarot card readings and talking to the dead. The narrator later recounts how Perla first met Darío in the shop and was enthralled by him, working at his side, learning how to run the store and the secrets to the various items he sold. When Darío left, Perla took over ownership of the shop even though she felt that she was not capable of running it, but it did fill the void inside of her that Guillermo had a hand in creating.

This chapter also fully introduces the reader to Rodrigo, a teenage boy who shows up at the shop alone and quite possibly on the run from immigration. Rodrigo's fate eventually becomes the ultimate test of faith for Perla, and perhaps the key turning point in the novel for the reader and their expectations of *Still Water Saints* as a magical-realist work. Later in the novel, the reader learns that Rodrigo had been brought to the United States as a sex slave and was held captive and abused. Given that Perla is a curandera, she turns to her mysticism in order to help him. First, she reads a particular passage to "the audience of Buddha and Shiva statues," but "they offered up no insights. No knowledge" (86). Shortly afterward, at a loss, she hears the voice of the now-dead Darío, who tells her to "feel it. . . . All of it. Use it. This santo here for this. That yerba there for that. Don't waste any part of it. All of it is precious and powerful. Like you, Perlita. Like you" (86).

These remedies, however, do not work—Rodrigo disappears and Perla is unable to find him, resulting in a complete crisis of faith. The narrator writes that "she had teas and colored veladoras and remedios scrawled on tattered index cards. *[Rodrigo] needed something else. And I didn't have a candle for it*" (205). If *Still Water Saints* were indeed a magical-realist novel, here it would likely hint at the expected surprise—that Rodrigo has turned up, perhaps worse for wear, but alive and safe and perhaps because of Perla's prayers and powers. However, the novel instead deals the reader an unexpected blow—the "badly burned" corpse of a young male is found on the banks of the Santa Ana River (207–8), and the only logical assumption is that it is indeed Rodrigo, given that the size of the body and age fits his description. Of all of the inhabitants of Agua Mansa that the reader meets in the novel, Rodrigo could easily be considered the most salient—his fate becomes a personal cause for Perla, and as a teenage boy caught in a poisonous web of sex trafficking, the reader roots for him to be saved. After all of the failed attempts at helping her customers up to this point in the novel, Rodrigo's fate also represents a narrative "last chance" for us to experience the power of the magical at the moment when it is needed the most. Because she fails, his death becomes the most astonishing unexpected surprise of the novel.

SURPRISE AS CHANGE

As I discussed earlier, surprise is theorized to lead to belief change—"the higher the level of surprise, the higher the probability that the agent will revise its knowledge" (Lorini and Castelfranchi 25). In the context of narrative, the implications for belief change are likely rather small in the case of the expected surprise. We may change our beliefs about what has actually transpired in a work in terms of plot, but so long as the work follows the conventions of a particular genre, the expected surprise is unlikely to change the schema that we have built for it. Returning to the hypothetical episode of *Law & Order*, when the guilty party is finally revealed to be somebody the viewer had previously dismissed, their perception of the events of that particular episode may change, but because this sort of "rug-pull" happens every episode, we fully expect this to happen. Thus, the twist is unlikely to change our perception of the genre as a whole, and indeed, if we piece together the clues of the episode, the surprise itself should have been postdictable.

It also stands to reason that if the crime featured in the *Law & Order* episode is particularly astounding, even in genres that rely upon the expected surprise, it may lead to belief change in real-world situations.[14] In the case of *Still Water Saints,* given that the reader

---

14. Clearly, when we speak of content rather than structure, and exclude surprise, fiction can and does result in belief change. This cognitive transfer between a work and a real-world situation is particularly important for those who discuss violence and sexuality in fictional representations. Many sustain that watching violence on television or in movies may encourage the spectator to become more violent, or have proviolent attitudes, which Funk et al. do find

has every reason to believe that the novel is indeed a magical-realist work, we would thus see two types of surprises in the novel, with corresponding levels of belief change. First, as the reader learns that Perla, a supposed curandera, likely does not have any magical powers or mystical connections and became a curandera only because she was a bored housewife, our perception of surprise toward further events in the novel may change. Toward the end of the novel, it may indeed become rather expected that Perla's "remedies" will not work. For example, when Nancy reveals that her father has slipped into a coma despite Perla's remedy, it is likely not surprising for the reader. Nor is it surprising that in "Charity," there will be no otherworldly repercussions for two young boys who steal a frequently blessed saint from the front of Perla's store. The impact of the final surprising event of the novel—when two young people are killed in an accident outside of Perla's store even after Lluvia paints a mural of Guadalupe to watch over the neighborhood—is also likely muted, even though the event itself is unexpected. In short, the "unexpected surprises" of the novel soon become expected because the novel conditions our schema toward this.

Nevertheless, for *Still Water Saints,* the larger implications come from the unexpected surprise it offers in terms of the genre as a whole—the unraveling of the "mystique" that is the hallmark of virtually all magical-realist works. As a body of work, Espinoza's novel is a mismatch with what many readers may perceive this genre to be, and it may well lead to a reevaluation of magic-realized novels in future readings. As such, the novel may manage to shift our genric schema—what could be considered belief change—assuming that the reader is not disappointed that the work does not offer them the "tasty" magical-realist experience that they are expecting, thus dismissing it entirely. Returning to Martín-Rodríguez's consideration

---

support for in younger people, but Rockoff rallies against in *The Rise and Fall of the Slasher Film*. On the other hand, for those who are not prone to committing violent acts, violence in media may make the spectator/audience more cautious or fearful in their everyday lives, with the expectation that the same sorts of events could happen to them. I discuss a similar concept in chapter 4 in regard to representations of homosexuals on television likely resulting in stronger acceptance of them in general society.

that Latinx literature has largely been linked to magical realism, *Still Water Saints* may offer a perfect entry point to change reader beliefs about this genre. It works to draw readers in who are looking for what fits that brand, but ends up offering them a very different reading experience strongly rooted in a modern reality.

So, if the novel does not reinforce the connection between Latinx literature and magical realism, what does it do? As many have noted, one of the hallmarks of Latinx production is its strong focus on the importance of family and community, instead of treating its protagonists as lone actors. Kanellos sees the struggle between individualism and family as recurring themes in Latinx immigrant works, as can be seen not only in well-known novels such as *The House on Mango Street* and *The Brief Wondrous Life of Oscar Wao* but also in the works of González, which I looked at in chapter 1. Interestingly, Muñoz's production does not seem to focus too much on the importance of family or community, instead portraying a series of isolated characters who find themselves in that circumstance for one reason or another. If we read *What You See in the Dark* and *Crossing Vines* in tandem, aside from the obvious differences in tone and style, in the first we see four female characters who become increasingly isolated from the world as the novel progresses, while the second focuses on the importance of creating a community in order to survive life in the grape fields. Even in *Butterfly Boy*, which portrays author González as feeling largely isolated, the reader is still aware that the author experiences an intense pull toward his family and community.

Kanellos also sees Latinx literature as generally exploring the pull of "materialism versus idealism and spirituality" (31),[15] and I

---

15. The point that Kanellos makes about materialism versus idealism and spirituality also resonates given that the community generally maintains its faith in Perla despite the fact that the botánica is clearly a commercial enterprise. In the first chapter, where Perla's "powers" are established, Espinoza also details how Perla cleans her store before closing shop and that she takes "inventory in her binder—noting that the candles were low, what packets of incense sticks had sold, what herbs and teas she was missing—and set the list next to the phone. *I'll place an order first thing tomorrow morning*" (10). This commercial aspect may come as an unexpected surprise for the reader—

believe that if we look at these two ideas in tandem, we arrive at the heart of what *Still Water Saints* truly attempts to accomplish. Even if Perla does not have the magic powers that the reader would initially assume that she does, for those in the community, she is a touchstone. For them, she really does "walk on water," and we see this in the multiple vignettes across the span of the novel. Even though Perla's remedy for Nancy's father does not work, she still returns to the botánica in the final chapter and at the end of the novel to purchase a candle for a vigil. When Perla apologizes that her previous remedy failed, Nancy "looked down at the ground and shook her head. 'It was too late by then. But you did all that you could. Thank you'" (234). When Perla goes to church during her crisis of faith, Father Madrid tells her: "Your store, it's important. . . . It's good for the community." In the final chapter of the novel, this point is driven further via a series of vignettes of people stopping by the shop. Even after her magic has been discredited in the eyes of the reader, Perla manages to calm down the mother of one of those killed in the motorcycle accident by giving her a rosary and telling her: "I can walk on water. The dead . . . Spirits and Saints. They talk to me. I just have to listen" (239). Later, the narrator writes: "Angela stopped crying and wiped her tears away as she held the rosary" (239). Thus, even though Perla does not have "powers," the mere belief that she does is a force that is beneficial to the community and its inhabitants.

Nevertheless, an aspect of the novel that may indeed be far more salient to the queer audience that is the focus of *Capturing Mariposas* is the creation of a space where community takes on a far more inclusive, modern meaning than we have typically seen in Latinx literature.[16] Perla feels herself becoming increasingly irrelevant, con-

---

although we know that these items must come from *somewhere*, they are not typically associated, at least so blatantly, with commercialism. Thus, although Perla and her store may represent idealism and spirituality for her customers, and perhaps the readers as well, there is a material base that underlies this, further strengthening the argument that her function as a community touchstone is her true importance in the novel. As a point of interest, in our interview Espinoza revealed that he included these aspects because of his own experience working at the retail store Hot Topic.

16. Espinoza's follow-up, *The Five Acts of Diego León,* calls to a queer audience even more than *Still Water Saints* given that the protagonist is gay and

fessing that her greatest fear is being forgotten and that she does not matter (67), so she transforms the botánica into an open, inclusive space where her primary goal is to help her customers, free of any judgment. An important example of this is found in transvestite Azúcar—although she believes that she passes well for a woman, there is a passage where she talks about how other women at the bus stop roll their eyes at her and snicker. Nevertheless, in Azúcar's two visits to the botánica, she encounters none of this snide attitude—although Perla does prod her about the baby that she brings into the store,[17] she does her best to fill Azúcar's spiritual needs.

This is just one example of how *Still Water Saints* creates Agua Mansa as a highly diverse location, contrasting strongly with the works of González and Muñoz that we saw in previous chapters. In Espinoza's world, the owner of the ninety-nine-cent store adjacent to the botánica is Asian, the donut shop is owned by Indians, Shawn is Caucasian, and Nancy's husband is African American, among others.[18] This diversity is treated very matter-of-factly in the novel, never becoming a plot point, further strengthening the botánica as an inclusive site of community. Overall, this demonstrates that although Agua Mansa (and by extension, innumerable other communities across the United States) has changed greatly, people like Perla still have relevance and importance given that they bind people together and create spaces of inclusion, reaffirming cultural schema of the importance of community. Tongson's 2011 study *Relocations: Queer Suburban Imaginaries*, which mentions *Still Water Saints* several times, looks at how several queer authors have "imagined" suburban Southern California as a place where "strange and wild things grow . . . where they shouldn't" (5). While this may be unsettling to a portion of the audience, particularly those who are comfortable in

---

comes to terms with that realization by the end of the novel. Although that novel does feature an interesting setting in both Mexico's War of the Cristeros and 1920s Hollywood, I find it less cohesive than Espinoza's debut, which is why I chose to exclude it from this book.

17. This is not Azúcar's baby. After watching a woman abandon him in front of the clinic where she works, she decides to take him instead of reporting the incident to the police.

18. Interestingly, the characters that seem to hold the most faith in Perla and the botánica are Latinx, and female in particular.

"suburbia's tidy yet nebulous sprawl" (5), it may provide hope to others—a vision of a place where they have a role to play. In many ways, we could even consider the botánica as the site of the same sorts of alternative kinship relations that Rodríguez explores in the introduction to his *Next of Kin*—a reconfiguration of familial kinship for the modern world.

RETURNING TO MAGICAL REALISM

The conclusion that *Still Water Saints* is really about the power of community and inclusion is not unique to my reading of the novel—in fact, reader reviews frequently mention that this is exactly what they enjoyed about the work. Deborah, a user on goodreads.com, wrote that "this story was like a web, with the old woman in the middle. . . . Each character is a crucial part of that web, part of a creation that is a world unto itself, a small drop of water in which I see everyone I've ever known reflected," while Mandolin commented that the novel made them "nostalgic for my botánica days and curse the fact that there is nowhere around here where one can buy a 7-day candle." Interestingly, few of the reviewers referenced the implied powers of Perla in the novel, which may indicate that many readers are able to look past the magic realization of the novel, an angle pushed by the publisher in the front cover and blurbs, by critics in reviews, and by Espinoza himself in the first chapter.

Although unarticulated, these reviews speak to the power of how *Still Water Saints*, through the use of cognitive surprise, effectively breaks down the borders of the apparent genre of the novel, perhaps transforming the reader's generic schema of similar Latinx literature in the process. Nevertheless, this consistent and unrelenting discrediting of Perla's magic in the novel is why the final paragraph of the novel may come as another surprise to the reader, as it did in my initial reading of the story. Here, Espinoza returns to a magical-realist bent—as the community gathers around the motorcycle accident scene, the narrator writes:

Perla and Angela added their candles to the rest, and the light from the veladoras grew. A yellow light rose up from the ground where they were clustered. It burst out in thick beams, shooting up to the sky, curving around the edges of buildings and houses and bending between tree branches and power lines, before it found its way back down. It descended upon them, and Perla watched as, one by one, they each shone bright, wiser and forever changed, stronger now. (240)

While this is certainly a beautiful piece of narrative to end the novel, it may come as one surprise too many for the reader, as it did for me. While the "light" could be figurative, speaking to the power of community, it is rather out of place in the rest of the novel. This scene is certainly not predictable, hence it being surprising for the reader, and is only postdictable if we discount much of what the novel has already related after the first chapter. Unfortunately, this closing may very well unwind some of the narrative surprises of the novel and the impact that it may have in transforming some audience perceptions of Latinx magical-realist literature.

CHAPTER 4

Market and Reader

IN THE INTRODUCTION I gave a few reasons for the importance of delineating a concrete genre of gay Chicano literature: as an organizing thread for the literature itself, and as a space of inclusion for readers to more easily find authors and works with which they identify. Thus far, I have mostly considered the role of authors in constructing this genre, exploring how Espinoza, González, and Muñoz challenge, reaffirm, and transform cultural schema primarily relevant to a gay Chicano readership. Nevertheless, any holistic study of genre construction, particularly looking at it from the realist perspective that I do here, would be incomplete if it did not leave space to consider publishing outcomes and reader reaction, which, as we will see, can be just as critical as the work itself: A genre needs publishers willing to back it, and an audience eager to consume it.

Turning first to publishers, they act as gatekeepers as to what sorts of gay Chicano experiences we see reflected on the written page and how they are packaged, a dynamic at the heart of the genric schema that I discussed in chapter 3. This gatekeeping, of course, is almost purely economic in nature—publishing houses exist to sell books and make money—and in this way, the impulse of genre itself can be viewed as an act of commodification undertaken to put a recognizable product in front of consumers. In academia, we tend not to think of the books as having an economic purpose or believe that the reason we have these books to study is because a given publisher believed there was a market for them. When we do take commodification under consideration, it tends to be viewed in a negative light—in terms of Latinx literature, we see these undertones in works such as Aldama's *Brown on Brown* and Martín-Rodríguez's *Life in Search of Readers*, to name just two studies that I have referenced in this book. Nevertheless, I see commodification as more ambiguous in nature; it can indeed have positive outcomes—particularly for new(er) authors in emerging genres—and considering reader responses to this literature can show us why.

LITERATURE AS PRODUCT

As we saw in the case of Espinoza's *Still Water Saints*, a good deal of thought and planning goes into "commodifying" literature. Putting myself in the mind-set of a publisher, here I am stripping away the artistic aspects of books, instead considering them as goods aimed at a particular audience and molded in such a way that consumers will notice and perhaps purchase them. As we saw in chapter 3, Bauman explains that goods offer the "straightforward sensual job of tasty eating, pleasant smelling, soothing or enticing drinking, relaxing driving, or the joy of being surrounded with small, glittering, eye-caressing objects" (50–51), and on its face, this may be reminiscent of a bookstore stacked with row upon row of colorful covers waiting to be bought and read, at least when these sites of literary capitalistic consumption were the primary means of purchasing literature. Nevertheless, Schwartz reminds us in *The Paradox of Choice* that having so many options can also be debilitating because, as he explains, we can become "overloaded" (2) and even paralyzed. Thus, while differentiation is important in order to grab the attention of a potential customer, it is also important for producers to create a "brand" so that the consumer knows, more or less, what to expect when they purchase that product.

To follow along with the cognitive analysis that has been critical to so much of this study, the act of branding lines up with the idea of genric schema that I have discussed throughout this book. Given our previous discussion of Hogan, we know that human memory tends to "cluster" similar experiences and lexicons into schemas, prototypes, and exempla (44). Thus, we can reasonably assume that consistent branding works to activate cognitive structures in a potential consumer so that they may link similar products together, which is particularly advantageous for the seller if the new product activates schema associated with a popular product already on the market. Although not focused on literature, Kreuzbauer and Malter look at embodied cognition and product design, writing that "design elements communicate information about the specific instrumentality of products and how people can physically interact with and use them" (166). They further add that "in this view, consumers perceive the type of action offered, or afforded, by physical features of the environment and the potential benefits afforded by products and brands," and that "such 'affordances' play an important role in consumer perception of products and brand categorization, i.e., how a product is perceived as a new member of a particular brand family (category)" (166). Affordances refer to how a person "can interact with" the product (166), which, in their case, would be whether a certain chair has the same utility for a short person as it does for a tall person.

Of course, books are not chairs, but I believe that we can treat them as consumer products all the same if they are branded as offering a certain type of reading experience, which is what Martín-Rodríguez explores in *Life in Search of Readers*. Leaning on his excellent work, here I will look at two aspects of the commodification of Latinx literature—covers and reviews[1]—how these work to fit

---

1. Martín-Rodríguez explores a third aspect—use of language—which is not entirely relevant to this conversation but is interesting nonetheless. In the general American literary market, books must be written in English in order to have wide appeal—it goes without saying that a monolingual Eng-

lish speaker would be unlikely to purchase a book with extensive dialogue in another language.

Nevertheless, we do know that much Latinx literature does incorporate at least some Spanish, and the way in which authors accomplish this is of particular interest to Martín-Rodríguez. As he explains, some critics have bemoaned the loss of linguistic diversity in Chicanx works that was prevalent in texts published during and immediately after the Chicano movement of the 1960s and 1970s, but his position is that this diversity has not disappeared, but has rather become stratified between two fronts, the *market* and *la marketa*, as he coins them. The market, which would include mainstream presses, tolerates little linguistic diversity within texts, while la marketa, consisting of "community readings, small press publications, and all kinds of locally distributed writings, still reflect[s] the linguistic diversity of earlier decades" (110). The split between these two markets occurred because earlier generations of Chicanx authors did not have publishing access to the market, meaning that they did not have to concern themselves with selling to a more mainstream, English-speaking audience. The author further explores the use of Spanish dialogue in works by Rechy and Islas, among others.

Given that Espinoza, González, and Muñoz have all been published in majority-English presses, we can easily consider their texts as written toward the market. The result of this is that they typically eschew linguistic diversity in their writing, but that does not mean that the characters in their works converse entirely in English. In *Still Water Saints,* while the reader is never entirely sure which language the characters are speaking, language use is referred to at several points. A scene in which Perla refuses to teach the young vagrant Rodrigo English because, as she insists, she never went to college and thus is not qualified (63) indicates that these characters probably speak Spanish to each other. It is worth noting that *Still Water Saints* was simultaneously published in Spanish as *Los santos de Agua Mansa, California.* Given the separation of language by edition, I would still make the argument that both titles were directed toward the market, not the marketa, and represent a push by Random House to reach more buyers, not to present a linguistically diverse but unified whole. Use of language is never truly an issue in Muñoz's works, but it is a factor in González's, primarily because his texts deal with characters and persons who most likely perform their daily lives in Spanish. Although it does not include much Spanish text, *Crossing Vines* does make references to the fact that some white characters are able to speak the language (46), that nobody in one character's particular family knew English very well (14), and that another women's "pocho" grandsons "weren't very popular with the crew because they spoke broken Spanish" (75), implying that everybody else converses primarily in that language. Similarly, *Butterfly Boy* also avoids the use of Spanish but does make frequent references to the fact that the author's first language is Spanish (12, 98) and compares Spanish and English as the young González is learning the latter (78).

Espinoza, González, and Muñoz into an already established brand of Latinx literature, and ultimately why we should not consider that a bad thing.

WEARING YOUR HEART ON YOUR (BOOK) SLEEVE

Up until a few years ago, the primary way that we bought literature was on foot—entering the bookstore for a particular title, or browsing until something grabbed our attention through its cover.[2] Martín-Rodríguez sees book covers as the most immediately noticeable place where the commodification of Latinx literature occurs, the result of the development of certain "brand appearance" that publishers have built up and maintained over the years, conditioning consumers to expect and look for it—essentially activating their generic schema of what Latinx literature "looks like." As he explains, covers frequently accentuate the childish, the naïve, and the colorful, with frequent use of pastel colors, which he terms the "tacobellization" of the Latinx image (131). In one example, he compares differences between the original edition of Ana Castillo's *The Mixquiahuala Letters* published by Bilingual Review Press, and a later edi-

---

For a nonspeaker of Spanish, there is also occasional dialog in English, which may appear strange, making it rather obvious that it is a direct translation from colloquial Spanish. For example, at times characters end sentences in "you"—for example, "I don't have enough money for class, you" (20). For a nonspeaker of Spanish, this is a rather strange way to end a sentence, indicating that the characters are probably not speaking English. Using *tú* at the end of a sentence, whether syntactically needed or not, is indeed a marker of rural Mexican Spanish.

2. It is impossible to overstate the importance of physical placement in a bookstore, given that extensive displays and prominent locations on endcaps do drive sales. Nevertheless, unless we speak of a novel by a best-selling author, it is unlikely to have a prominent enough placement that that would be the deciding factor in whether or not a reader notices the book's presence. Espinoza's *Still Water Saints* certainly fits into this unknown author category— although published by Random House, he was a new author at the time of publication, and given the relative paucity of reviews found online, it likely did not receive a huge promotional push by the company. While Muñoz appears to be more well-known, he is still not a best seller and González, printed mostly by university presses, likely did not figure in corporate bookstores at all.

tion by Doubleday. As he writes, the first "is austere, in blue, black, and gray tones, with just one image of what looks like a sheet of paper . . . By contrast, the Doubleday edition has opted for a much more colorful cover in which reproductions of Mexican lottery cards . . . are arranged around the cover," which he believes implies that the book is from a Mexican author, not an American one (132).

While these sorts of differences are readily evident in a works like Castillo's that have been published in multiple presses, we can still observe some of the same practices in the covers of Espinoza, González, and Muñoz. Muñoz's works tend to fit the least into this defined "Latinx" brand, perhaps with the exception of his first, *Zigzagger,* which does use a green pastel coloring, centered upon a hand holding a card with the title "Zigzagger." *The Faith Healer of Olive Avenue* and *What You See in the Dark* deviate far from this brand, particularly the latter, with its black-and-white film-noir-inspired graphics, fitting well with the tone and plot of the story itself. This is perhaps not unexpected, given that this particular novel does not have the Chicanx community as its primary subject and represents Muñoz's foray into producing a general market novel. In short, there is not a whole lot that could be branded "Latinx" about this work aside from the author himself and one of the main characters, and publisher Algonquin Press does not seem to try to force fit it into that category.

With González, we can see far more of this branding influence. *Crossing Vines,* whose colorful graphics depict people working in the fields, may be reminiscent of Mexican muralist Diego Rivera's works for the informed consumer, while González's more recent works, *Autobiography of My Hungers* and *Our Lady of the Crossword,* both rely on pastel and indigenous-influenced images for their covers. In Espinoza's *Still Water Saints,* we see the graphics that perhaps best fit the magic-realized brand that I discussed in chapter 3: In pastel tones, the upper body of a young woman floats in the sea, while what looks to be a lily pad sits in the lower corner. This image has almost nothing to do with the content of the book itself—the woman is certainly not the curandera Perla, who is more than seventy years old. Meanwhile, the choppy sea drawn is contrary to the state of the titular water, and furthermore Agua Mansa, the location of the story, is described to be located around Riverside, California, not near any body of water. Nevertheless, the cover is striking, at once fitting the Latinx brand, but also standing out in its simplicity. As Espinoza revealed in his interview, he was ultimately satisfied with it, particularly after rejecting one in which Perla was "standing over the town, giant, and she's releasing all of these charms. She had rays, like the Virgin Mary does, around her, and she had a ponytail. They said we think that this is going to make for a really striking cover and it's going to be awash in warm Mexican colors." He candidly described it as "absolutely atrocious."

REVIEWING MAGIC

Apart from the cover, reviews and blurbs on the back cover were also a very important area to grab potential readers in the bookstore setting, and still are to some extent. As Martín-Rodríguez explains, in commodified Latinx literature, these areas also work to reinforce the brand, particularly if there is any connection to magical realism. In the terms of Kreuzbauer and Malter, we may consider these affordances, allowing readers to contrast and compare texts within the same genre. Martín-Rodríguez observes that reviewers have tended to accentuate the "magical" qualities of a text, even going as far as an "obligated" reference to Gabriel García Márquez (126), a comparison that Espinoza also revealed that he has inexplicably received. In their blurbs found at the back of a book, even Latinx authors themselves may fall into this trap and use wording in reviews that they know will grab the attention of publishers and editors and wind up being published (124).

The blurbs on the back cover of *Still Water Saints* frequently fall into this trap. Sandra Cisneros offers up the first (and most cited on websites such as Amazon), calling the novel "a cycle of tales as perfect as the beads on a rosary. One alone is a little miracle; the whole together is capable of renewing one's faith in new fiction." The review says virtually nothing about the content of the work itself, but it does evoke the images of both the rosary and a miracle, conjuring up the idea of mysticism that Martín-Rodríguez cites in several of the reviews that he looks at. The *Washington Post* uses both "magic" and "faith" in its two-line blurb, while the *San Francisco Chronicle* believes that the novel is "enchanting" and that it "bewitches." In terms of reviews, that of *Entertainment Weekly* would make it seem like Perla actually has mystical powers; it categorizes the novel under "Fiction" and "Occult and Paranormal" (Lee). For their part, neither the blurbs on the covers of González's nor Muñoz's works push the idea that they are "magical"—González's tend to be straightforward, focusing on aspects of the works themselves, while Muñoz's frequently evoke dark and erotic images, appropriate for the stories that he tells.

COMMODIFICATION, GOOD AND BAD

As noted, I tend to view commodification more ambiguously than many other studies, but its negatives are clear to see, including those already outlined. This commodification is also a detriment to new authors; it has been suggested that the market views Latinx literature as a niche to fill and profit from without putting real work into developing the next generation. As Aldama writes, some publishers may pick up a work by a Latinx author, then not look for any others because that market has been "served" (*Brown* 93).[3] Unfortunately for newer authors, this results in a reification of the Latinx literature best-sellers list, something that can be seen at Amazon.com. Although the company notes that their list of Hispanic American bestsellers is updated hourly, there is very little movement in the overall rankings, and older, established literature tends to dominate

---

3. In regard to the scant number of Latinx authors picked up by large publishing firms, Aldama writes that "this is precisely how capitalism works: first by heterogenizing and then by homogenizing cultural phenomena" (*Brown* 93). It is important to note here that both Aldama and Martín-Rodríguez specify that the content that a good deal of these Latinx authors have produced has *not* been homogenized, despite market forces.

sales. When I was originally writing this section during the last few months of 2012, Junot Díaz's *The Brief Wondrous Life of Oscar Wao* (2007) and *This Is How You Lose Her* (2012) and Cisneros's *The House on Mango Street* (1984) were consistently listed as top three sellers, while other familiar names, including Esmeralda Santiago and Julia Álvarez, dominated the top ten positions. Furthermore, the average age of the works on this list was twelve years old during the same period of study, while all of the works on the general "American" literature list were published within the past several months. Six years later, Cisneros's, Díaz's, and Álvarez's older books *still* dominate the top positions, with newer entries appearing for perhaps a week or two before dropping off.[4] Tying this into Aldama's observation, because these established authors and works are still dominating sales, there may be little incentive for large publishing firms to pick up or promote new authors, and the ones that are picked up may have that luck because they fit somewhere within the already established market, or have similarities to another popular Latinx (or Latin American) author.

Nevertheless, commodification does carry with it certain benefits, and we could even say that it is because of this treatment that some Latinx literature has gone mainstream, reaching broad audiences. Junot Díaz's novel *The Brief Wondrous Life of Oscar Wao* spent more than thirty weeks on the *New York Times* best-sellers list, a feat that no other Latinx work had accomplished up to that point, although Rechy's *City of Night* came close, at twenty-five weeks upon its release in 1963. Other works have become best sellers and boast deep cultural penetration, such as Sandra Cisneros's debut *The House on Mango Street*, which has been incorporated into the curriculums of schools across the United States. Even if they do not share *Oscar Wao*'s immediate sales success, perhaps they do not need to. As Anne Messitte, publisher of Vintage Español explains, many Latinx works

---

4. Here I purposefully exclude some works of literature that have appeared on this list. At some point between 2013 and 2015, Amazon changed their algorithm so that this "best sellers" list now includes romance novels. Candidly speaking, I have no idea if the authors are Latinx, as some go by pseudonyms, or whether these books are classified as "Hispanic" merely because of their content.

have a "Long Tail," meaning that even if they have small shipments during the week of their respective releases, they may continue to sell at a steady pace for long periods. In an interview with the *New York Times* in 2002, Messitte explained that "it's not unusual to ship fewer than 10,000 copies and then be up to 30,000 by the twelfth month" (Arnold). Works that fall into this category are almost too innumerous to mention, but would certainly include Cisneros's debut,[5] as well as Anaya's *Bless Me, Ultima,* both of which have been described as the best-selling Chicanx novels of all time. Writ large, absent the commodifying impulse contorting works to fit certain schematic parameters, it likely would have been more difficult for these books to reach significant cross sections of the general public. At the same time, artistic purity need not come at the expense of putting books into the hands of more readers. We can consider recent magical-realist works as trite, but we have also seen in the case of Espinoza how its genric schema can be used as a tool to become published even when the literature itself works to subvert the genre. In this way, although the homogenizing tendency of commodification is not preferable, neither is it necessarily negative.

TRANSCULTURATION, GENRE, AND SEXUALITY

Given that a number of Latinx authors have indeed achieved broad market penetration, it appears that they have become adept at creating texts that are being read both within and outside of their home communities. As Martín-Rodríguez explains, "transcultural Chicana/o literature often includes what could be defined as an anthropologi-

---

5. As Martín-Rodríguez notes, critic Ellen McCracken "denounced the lack of mainstream critical and popular attention accorded to . . . *The House on Mango Street*" (129). In her 1989 article, McCracken wrote that it was "difficult to find in most libraries and bookstores" ("Sandra" 63). These words were written a full five years after the novel had first been published by Arte Público, demonstrating how long it took for the novel to "catch on" among a wider audience.

cal or ethnographic discourse that becomes a cultural explanation of sorts for the benefit of the distant readers" (116), similar to how Kim sees treatment of Maxine Hong Kingston's *The Woman Warrior* as a "buffet style approach to discrete, exoticized cultures" (105). In effect, this recreates these authors as cultural ambassadors, an idea Martín-Rodríguez ties into Rama's theory of narrative transculturation (113–14). Borrowing from others, particularly the Cuban anthropologist Fernando Ortiz, Rama used this theory to explain how some writers were able to create unified visions of diverse worlds that often inhabited the same territory, such as Peruvian author José María Arguedas, part indigenous and part *criollo*. Regarding transculturation, Rama explained:

> The concept of transculturation is . . . articulated along a dual verification. On one hand, it registers that the present culture of the Latin American community . . . is composed of idiosyncratic values which are acknowledged as asserting influence since the remotest of times. On the other hand, the process of *transculturation* corroborates the creative energy that powers Latin American culture, making it very distinct from a simple aggregate of norms, behaviors, beliefs and objects. (136)[6]

Rama, in turn, used this theory to explain how an author such as Arguedas was able to write novels such as *Los ríos profundos* and the unfinished *El zorro de arriba y el zorro de abajo*, both of which combine indigenous and Western religions and languages. However,

---

6. It is important to note that Rama's work is not without criticism; Antonio Cornejo Polar has written that "*transculturation* would imply, in the long run, the construction of a syncretic plane that finally incorporates, in a more or less unproblematic totality (in spite of the conflictive character of the processes), two or more languages, two or more ethnic identities, two or more aesthetic codes and historical experiences" (117). If we consider Chicanx literature, it would seem that Cornejo Polar's own theory of heterogeneity, in which "discontinuous discourses are generated within heterogeneous stratifications that, in a certain way, fragment and hierarchize history" (118) would likely be more applicable.

these works were also clearly written with a larger, majority Spanish-speaking market in mind, and this can be observed in the author's personal diaries included in *El zorro*. Given the continuing popularity of his works and the sheer number of scholarly studies they have engendered, one can easily say that Arguedas was successful in articulating this indigenous worldview to the Spanish-speaking majority.[7]

As we have seen, there is undoubtedly a homogenizing influence exerted over much Latinx literature in order to fit into an already defined market. Nevertheless, even genre-bending works such as *Oscar Wao* hold an advantage over Espinoza, González, and Muñoz given that they are largely heteronormative in nature, and thus are not completely foreign to a mainstream audience. In a Latinx literature class where I taught both Díaz's novel and Reinaldo Arenas's *Before Midnight*, most students seemed completely comfortable reading the first, but others demonstrated unease with the second. Both contain explicit details that delve into human sexuality, but Díaz's novel is almost oppressively heteronormative, while *Before Midnight* is clearly not. Though both authors likely become cultural ambassadors for certain cross sections of Latinx through their writing, it is unlikely that Díaz comes to represent all heterosexuals in the

---

7. Although successful, Arguedas personally was tortured, and ended his own life in 1969. His final diaries, included with *El zorro*, indicate a disillusionment particularly with the writing establishment in Latin America, including a personal dislike for Alejo Carpentier, Mario Vargas Llosa, Julio Cortázar, and Carlos Fuentes, the first of whom, he wrote, seems to view "our indigenous things to be an excellent element or [raw] material to work with" (14). This criticism would seem, at least in spirit, to be similar to the one made by Chicana feminists of their Euro-American counterparts. In *This Bridge Called My Back*, the introduction to the chapter "Racism in the Women's Movement" calls this out rather clearly: "In academic and cultural circles, Third World women have become the subject matter of many literary and artistic endeavors by White women, and yet we are refused access to the pen, the publishing house, the galleries, and the classroom" (Moraga and Anzaldúa 61). In a 1991 interview, Castillo further clarified this, explaining that she feels a closer connection with other women of color than with "Anglo feminists" (Torres 156). Cotera examines the historical struggles between Chicana and Anglo feminists—the former, she writes, had "little or no support from Anglo colleagues" (215), while *Chicana Feminist Thought*, the anthology in which Cotera's essay appears, contains an entire section devoted to examining the gaps between these two factions.

way that Arenas becomes a proxy for homosexuals. This is precisely where we find one of the challenges of forming gay Chicano literature as a genre in the context of the mainstream publishing world. These authors are essentially attempting a transculturation of two literary worlds—queer and Latinx—that do not have a strong history of harmonious coexistence.

In the case of Espinoza and Muñoz, the commodificational response to this transculturation has been extraordinary contortions to avoid any mention of their gayness on their book covers. In the case of Espinoza's *Still Water Saints,* this may be understandable given that it does not feature a great deal of queer representation, but his subsequent novel, *The Five Acts of Diego León* (2013), not only deals with a young Mexican who goes to Hollywood to embark on an acting career in the 1920s but is also about a protagonist who struggles and ultimately comes to terms with his homosexuality, a plot essential to the conclusion of the work. Nevertheless, aside from Cisneros mentioning that it breaks taboos of "race and sexuality," the book jacket summary only reveals that Diego finds that "the past is not so easily escaped, as he is drawn again and again to the painful legacy of history and the wounds of his homeland." Meanwhile, Muñoz's *Zigzagger* and *Faith Healer,* both of which feature a bevy of gay protagonists, make little effort to reach this audience in their respective blurbs and summaries. It appears that only González can be openly gay in this market, perhaps unavoidable given the subject matter that he tackles. The titles of the books themselves—*Butterfly Boy, Mariposa Gown,* and so on—also contain conspicuous gay connotations. Perhaps González's affinity toward smaller and university presses has allowed him the latitude to openly identify as a gay author in these areas—in effect, that has become his branding. Nevertheless, this speaks to the difficulty of putting together gay Chicano literature as a genre when some of its authors are being published in presses that seem to eschew mention of their sexuality, as if gay and Latinx branding are mutually exclusive.

Nevertheless, there are important counterpoints to this observation—both John Rechy and Michael Nava have had long, successful careers in presses both big and small producing works that are eminently identifiable as both gay and Chicano, although that coexistence has not always been harmonious. Despite the overwhelming success of Rechy's *City of Night*, it was for many years rejected by the Chicanx literary canon because it "didn't focus on ethnicity or satisfy the political vision of the Chicano movement" (Torres 18). In his 1978 article, Paredes essentially argues that *City of Night* is not Chicano enough to be included (104)—the protagonist's ethnic identity is not mentioned—and we see echoes of this argument in the feedback that Muñoz received for his novel *What You See in the Dark* more than thirty years later.[8] Meanwhile, in an interview with Aldama, Nava recalls numerous rejections during the mid-1980s that he believes stemmed from his protagonist, Henry Ríos, being a gay Chicano. He also credits a wave for some of his success later in that decade and into the 1990s—"gay became more fashionable"—allowing him to break into the New York publishing scene and eventually land with mass-market Penguin Putnam (Aldama, *Spilling* 194).

Arturo Islas was not as successful, however—he recounted to Torres the difficulties he encountered in publishing his 1984 debut *The Rain God* in its original form, *Día de los muertos / Day of the Dead* (Torres 69), and Aldama notes that the final version was "greatly trimmed of its original . . . queer characterization" by the publisher (*Brown* 112). In some way, we may be able to consider texts by Espinoza, Muñoz, and even Islas as acts of resistance not only against the heteronormative communities these authors come from but also against the largely heteronormative book market in which they have published. That said, an often underconsidered benefit of commodification is reach: Even given its problems, mass marketing does put books into the hands of readers or at least give this literature exposure that it may not have achieved otherwise. For an genre such as gay Chicano literature that has not yet carved out its own identifiable market niche, that reach is critical. In the case of *Diego León* or *Faith Healer* (or Islas's *The Rain God*), even if the publisher has taken easily identifiable efforts to obfuscate their queer content, they still published the book, affording them at least a fair chance at connecting

---

8. See chapter 5.

with a wider audience than they may have gotten at a smaller press, if they were published at all.

HEARTS AND MINDS: READER EXTERNALIZATIONS

As I mentioned earlier, exploring how readers externalize what they have read—acting on the politics inherent in these works—can show us why the commodifying impulse can be beneficial if it results in more exposure. Nevertheless, we know that the audience is not a homogenous entity—even if the book is read by more people, that does not mean that they will all *do* something with its rhetoric. In considering these political implications, here I model for three different readerships rooted in the idea of potential for change, backed up by real reader sentiment that I have found both online and in my own classrooms: those who are sympathetic/ empathetic to the characters that González, Espinoza, and Muñoz create; those who may be inclined to be sympathetic/empathetic although they may not have considered their lives before reading these works; and finally, those who reject any sympathetic/empathetic feeling whatsoever. Although virtually all of González's works contain clear messages about both gays and Latinx, here I will focus on the implications of the two works that I explored in chapter 1, *Crossing Vines* and *Butterfly Boy*. Muñoz's works are not as overtly political as those of González, but the two collections of short stories do feature a variety of gay characters who likely challenge reader sentiment. I will also include Espinoza's second novel, *The Five Acts of Diego León*, in this discussion, given its strong gay content.

As we see above, I also return to the idea of sympathy and empathy discussed in chapter 1 because it has strong transformative political implications that vague narration and surprise may not. According to many scholars, sympathy and empathy work to bring the audience closer to the point of view of the subject in order to understand their circumstance. For example, Trout writes that "empathy is alert to the humiliation and indignity of being treated differently for reasons that are morally irrelevant, such as race or class" (17), which I believe speaks to its power. Furthermore, because of the transformative rhetoric of empathy and sympathy, I believe that many readers would find it difficult to ignore the politics of these works, as enjoyable as they may be as self-contained narratives.

Part of the problem with sympathy and empathy in literature is that, as Keen reminds us, the reader cannot offer the characters aid as they might in the real world ("Narrative Empathy" 70). What readers can do, however, is apply what they feel for fictional characters to like groups in the real world, which is where the political implications of literature arise. As I discussed in chapter 1, in her analysis of *The Woman Warrior*, Kim sees this conflation of characters and their real-life counterparts as problematic for a number of reasons, but many readers seem to do so regardless, as many of my students did with *Crossing Vines*. In chapter 2, I briefly discussed Zunshine's theorization of "cognitive slippage," where, at least in the moment of reading, we may not distinguish between real people and fictional characters (*Why We Read* 19). So, while we may know that these characters are not real in an abstract sense, a politically minded reader is also likely aware that they are not drawn out of thin air—somewhere out there, real people like them *do* exist and suffer in similar ways, and for this reason, it becomes important to study what the larger implications of these works may be.

I UNDERSTAND HOW YOU FEEL

Studies into the effects of sympathy and empathy generally agree that when these literary techniques are successful, they may produce a "proattitude" or "prosocial" behavior (Eisenberg and Eggum 71; Singer 20). However, for readers who are already sympathetic/empathetic toward the plight of gays, or migrant workers in the case of *Crossing Vines*, it hardly matters because these works are unlikely to make readers feel less for these groups. For some readers, it may be because they identify with González, his father, the characters of

Zigzagger, or the closeted Diego León. Hoffman, for example, uses the term "empathetic bias" to describe situations in which a person is more likely to feel empathy for those "like them," and less likely to feel so, or at least to feel less strongly, for those who are different (67). Similarly, Wispé observes that "we groups" may form, which entails a feeling of kinship, although she notes that this positioning is complicated by the "determinants of similarity" in empirical testing" (74–76). Trout, meanwhile, writes that we are more inclined to help people we know, or people like them, "because our experience with them decreases the social distance between us" (36).

Nevertheless, identification does not necessarily need to occur. Carroll, for example, writes of "solidarity" with protagonists in narrative texts, particularly when these characters are morally good (175). In turn, "antagonists instill anger, indignation, hatred, and sometimes even moral disgust in us" (176). In *Crossing Vines,* the reader may feel this resentment toward the mechanisms of dominant society, particularly those who are racist toward Chela and her children (52), or toward the police, who shot and killed Moreno with little reason (149), but probably not toward Lozano, the owner of the grape field who also received a sympathetic turn, as described in chapter 1.[9] The difficult upbringing of Diego León, set against the backdrop of the Mexican Revolution, and his fight against his own sexuality during a time when it was not acceptable to be gay, is also likely to inspire such feelings of solidarity in the willing reader. In "Monkey Sí" from *Zigzagger,* Muñoz leads us to feel this moral disgust for Tomás while feeling protective over Nestor, who is on

---

9. While in *Crossing Vines* the reader may feel solidarity with just about everybody due to the way in which González lays out the narrative, *Butterfly Boy* is much more ambiguous as there are few true antagonists in the biography. As discussed earlier, one could consider the author's father the antagonist, but that is not likely given that he is, many times, also portrayed as a victim. González's grandfather could also be seen as an antagonist, but he is not pitted sufficiently against the author to truly see him that way. Instead, I believe that feelings of solidarity in *Butterfly Boy* would likely fall along the lines of the father/son, as discussed in terms of empathy in that chapter.

the receiving end of both emotional abuse and a brutal rape that destroys their relationship.

Wispé also describes a much more disingenuous form of sympathy, which I label "selfish vindication." For the author, such a form of sympathy may entail a martial-arts expert helping out a person in distress, but doing so more to demonstrate their skills than out of a feeling of duty (70). In the case of *Crossing Vines,* for example, this type of sympathetic reader may get a perverse sense of joy out of how the migrant workers suffer, if only because it reinforces their views that these workers are treated unfairly or caught in an unjust system. This returns to Tan's idea of pleasure in the manipulation of reader emotion, discussed in chapter 1, and perhaps even Bauman's concept of consumerism and "tasty" reading. While there still exists the idea of solidarity with these people/characters, it is also somewhat self-serving, such as in the case of Leonardo in *Crossing Vines*. In *Diego León,* the lengths to which the protagonist goes to deny his own sexuality may also engender this sort of selfish vindication among readers who see him as an example of how queer people have suffered historically. In all of these cases, readers already have a predisposition toward feeling empathy/sympathy when reading these works as a part of their already established embedded schema that they bring with them, and while the author's direction of the text may intensify these feelings, it is unlikely to change the political opinions of the readers.

NOW I UNDERSTAND HOW YOU FEEL

The second type of readership that I envision for these works is perhaps the most important: those who may be inclined toward feeling sympathy and/or empathy but had not really considered the plight of the characters before picking up these books. In terms of schema, to call upon Moya, these readers may have held poorly defined schema of these politics and not even realized it (*Social* 24). As noted, many theorize that sympathy and empathy lead to prosocial behavior; Galloway-Thomas, for example, considers empathy as crucial to "addressing intercultural issues" (4), seeing it giving the subject the ability to "enter into and participate in the world of the cultural Other cognitively, affectively, and behaviorally" (8). As she further notes, Hochschild pinpoints empathy as the reason for the abolishment of slavery in the British empire, as white abolitionists exposed ordinary Britons to the harsh practices behind the products that they consumed (12). Similarly, Hoffman outlines an idea of "empathetic injustice," which focuses on the victim's plight, but only if that plight is perceived as "not deserved" (56). He also observes that empathy can, over time, change attitudes (65), and furthermore, that moral dilemmas may arise because of it (66). Empathy has also been tied to democracy, which Morrell defines as a "deliberation that puts empathy at its heart" because of the need to "give citizens equal consideration" (159). In considering these last two points, we can point to local elections in many American states to ban same-sex marriage in the 2000s as a case where empathy and morality may create a dilemma, particularly for the religious faithful who may also know queers in their everyday lives. The question here is whether or not a sense of empathy for these "cultural others" is able to overcome some sense of religious duty when they cast their ballots.

In some cases we may see acts of altruism, an important concept in discussions of sympathy and empathy. On a basic level, Singer writes that human beings have an innate sense of fairness and are generally altruistic, "whether because he feels for the other or because he has a sense of social justice" (25), while van Lange et al. see empathy as generating generosity in clinical experiments, even when it has a personal cost to the empathizer, something generally agreed to be altruistic in nature (101). Shott sees empathy when sharing negative emotions, such as shame or guilt, as motivating a person to alleviate the burden of the other and to prove themselves as "morally adequate" (1327). Thus, the political function of *Crossing Vines* or *Diego León* for this group of readers would be to open their minds to "others" whom they may have previously thought negatively of, or not considered at all—to see them as sympathetic/empathetic humans—which might perhaps lead to prosocial behavior on behalf of their real-life counterparts, up to and including acts of altruism. Of course, what sorts of altruistic acts may result are too numerous to present here and would depend on the specific reader, but in an age where rights of the LGBT community and migrant workers are still hot-button political fodder, changing hearts and minds of individuals is an important way to win battles.[10]

It is important to note here that most of this research on empathy/sympathy, prosocial behavior, and altruism are speaking of real-life, face-to-face situations. What role is there for fiction in generating these feelings? When US vice president Joe Biden came out in favor of same-sex marriage in May of 2012, he cited NBC sitcom *Will & Grace* (1998–2006, 2017–) as a milestone in gay acceptance, particularly given that at its peak, it was watched by upwards of 20 million viewers a week and generated little controversy. This series led the way for gay characters to become a staple in American television programming, to the point where a gay or lesbian character is no longer a notable occurrence. Here, I specifically use the example of television series because they have a much wider reach than literature, particularly works such as those of González that have not appeared on any best-sellers lists. Nevertheless, changing hearts and minds on issues such as gays' and migrant workers' rights is a battle often fought on an individual basis, meaning that works by Espinoza, González, and Muñoz do have an important role to play.

I'LL NEVER UNDERSTAND HOW YOU FEEL

Before turning toward the audience that would reject any sort of sympathy and/or empathy for the characters that Espinoza, González, and Muñoz sketch, I return to the idea of the implied readership of the text discussed in chapter 1. There are a number of different points of view among narratologists regarding who exactly composes the

---

10. There are two important caveats here. First, Miller writes that in cases of potentially altruistic acts, the observer may ask why it is their responsibility to help (107). This is an important point to consider, and some may feel that it is not their responsibility, or worse, as we will see later among the overheard audience. Seglow, among others, also advances the idea that altruistic acts must contain some cost to those who perform them (145). I do not entirely agree with this assertion; one could argue that casting a ballot in favor of same-sex marriage is an altruistic act that carries no cost whatsoever to those who do so.

message of the text: the author or the reader. These would seem to map closely to Iser's two poles of the text—the artistic, formed by the author, and the aesthetic, formed by the reader. Iser writes that both are of equal importance because "the text only takes on life when it is realized. . . . The convergence of text and reader brings the literary work into existence," adding that this realization is never exact, or at least cannot be studied as such (*Act* 274–75). Iser also sees the potential text—the convergence—as infinitely rich (280) because the reader provides the unwritten part of the text and the author never sets down the entire picture (282). Because each reader is different and the author intentionally leaves space for interpretation, this configuration implies there are as many possible configurations of meanings as there are readers.

This assumes that all views are created equal, but Fish does not believe that to be the case. He defines an "informed reader" and maintains that if a member of the audience does not share the central concerns of a work, they are not capable of responding to it (50). The idea of the intended/represented reader would seem to fall somewhat within the line of thinking of Fish, meaning that the author is likely directing a work to a specific audience that shares its embedded cultural schema, but this does not necessarily mean that readers not in this audience do not have access to it. García Landa, for his part, labels this audience, those outside of the intended/represented readership, as "unintended readers," and believes that they "overhear" texts and make meaning of them as well (192). He also explains that some will be able to identify with the implied readership even if they do not belong to it, while others may simply remain "eavesdroppers" (204).

Who might be the overheard audience of works such as those by Espinoza, González, and Muñoz? In chapter 1, I suggested that the intended audience of *Crossing Vines* would be one that sees the grape pickers as victims of circumstance without agency, leading to the didactic message that these characters (and people) are worthy of respect, not mere pity. In *Butterfly Boy*, meanwhile, I see both a homosexual and heterosexual intended readership, bound together through the idea of empathy and catharsis. In Muñoz, I would peg the intended audience generally as Latinx, particularly given the lack of signifiers on the cover, in the blurbs, and in the summary that his collections are gay-focused. Espinoza's *Diego León* is categorized as gay literature on Amazon.com, but it would also be attractive to those with interest in the Mexican Revolution or the early film industry. If we consider the view of García Landa in conjunction with the idea of the intended readership, we may very well see members of this "overheard audience"—those not among these intended audiences—who end up feeling sympathy/empathy for the characters portrayed. In this case, the political implications of these works are strongly realized.

Nevertheless, we must also keep in mind that there is an overheard audience that does not feel either of these two responses, and reader reviews on goodreads.com offers a number of vivid examples.[11] Although *Butterfly Boy* has garnered overwhelmingly positive reviews on the website, there are a few readers who clearly were not won over by González's narrative technique. User Yasmin writes that she did not understand why the author "blame[d] everything on his father. A father that was by no means perfect, but there seemed to be something missing." As discussed in chapter 1, González seems to recognize this himself in the autobiography, which is why he has such a conflictive relationship with his father in the first place—he blames everything on him, but perhaps knows that he should not. Here, it is difficult to judge empathy and/or sympathy; however, this reader is likely among the overheard audience who has perhaps not experienced dynamics similar to those of González and his father. Another reader on the same website left a scathing review, stating, "I don't know if I ever will finish. I get tired of self-righteous or pitiful authors. I am sorry you are gay and people don't understand you. . . . I just can only be empathetic to a certain extent!" (Renee). This reader is clearly among the overheard audience that rejects González's empathetic union, recalling Clark's idea of sympathy credits that was discussed in chapter 1. For this reader, González has used up all of his credits, and they will not extend more.

---

11. There may very well be readers who fall within the intended audience who also reject these characters for their own reasons. When we speak of real readers instead of prototypical intended readers, the study becomes much more complex and difficult to demonstrate on a theoretical basis.

In the case of *Diego León,* one reader on goodreads.com was clearly a part of the overheard audience, although not for lack of sympathy or empathy. As I noted earlier, there is very little on the cover or in the blurbs or reviews that would indicate that the protagonist's struggle with his sexuality is an overarching theme of the novel. For Salem, this in itself was problematic, which points to a failure in how the novel was commodified by Random House. She writes:

> Being latina, i was expecting a book with history on a mexican born person having to assimilate to the american culture. Not just American culture, but also Hollywood culture. I thought it made for an interesting book, at least it could have been. Instead, the book focused on Diego's sexuality. I am not the slightest agains homosexuality, but reading some parts of this book made me very uncomfortable. Overall, no one in the book club liked this book because we were each expecting something different.

Returning to sympathy and empathy, readers do not necessarily even need to like these characters in order to feel for them, as we see in the case of *Butterfly Boy,* where González is at times very critical of himself but still elicits sympathy from a wide number of readers. For *Diego León,* Esmeralda on goodreads.com found the protagonist himself very unlikeable, although she notes that "it did make me stop and think about how much a person may suffer when they don't accept them self just the way they are," presumably referring to his sexuality. This is an important consideration in Muñoz's works, as his hallmark is conflicted, ambiguous gay characters who may not be very likeable at all. We see this prominently in "Monkey Sí," as well as in a number of other gay characters involved in shady dealings, like the drug addict son in "The Unimportant Lila Parr."

Again, different readers may take different messages away from the same book. There may be readers who are potentially sympathetic to the plight of undocumented workers but are repelled by Chela's abrasive attitude, or who may consider González as overly self-absorbed in *Butterfly Boy.* It is impossible to model for every potential readership, which is why I have attempted to pare it down to three basic archetypes here.

Returning to the introduction of this book and the idea of reader identification with literature, it is also critical to discuss where gay Chicano readers—those who likely share the cultural schema embedded within these works—may fall. Readers like Alvarez likely form part of the already sympathetic audience, and this is something we clearly see in his recounting of discovering Cuadros's *City of God*—given that these works express their subjectivities as both queers and Chicanos, these readers would likely be empathetic to the characters and situations drawn. We may also see these readers fall into the newly sympathetic audience, particularly if these works help them come to terms with their own sexuality or consider their relatives in a different light, as we see in the example of *Butterfly Boy*. Nevertheless, it is important to remember that a reader may not identify with a work solely because it reflects their own subjectivity and life experiences. Here I can cite the example of the American television remake of *Queer as Folk*—theoretically, I should have identified with its characters, but in reality, I found them poorly drawn and utterly unlikeable to a large extent. In this case, while an audience member may identify with characters and situations, they may reject a work entirely out of personal preference and taste.

MAKING THE MARKET

Earlier in this chapter, I wrote about how the commodification of literature has the potential to put works into more hands, but this view may be problematic as it puts readers at the mercy of publishing houses to make this literature available to them and to organize it in a way that is recognizable as a genre. While this may have been true in the past, particularly when the only way to buy books was in a bricks-and-mortar store, now more than ever readers possess the ability to intervene in the market in ways that were previously impossible, putting their own spin on the commodifying impulse. In an abstract way, readers have always been capable of this based on their purchasing habits—retailers and publishers chase customers, and their tastes determine what is carried, and where. However, as we also know, many times it is not that simple. Martín-Rodríguez and Aldama have both shown how many Chicanx authors have historically been cut off from access to publishers, much less entry into prominent book retailers. A further complication for the gay Chicano voices that I study here is that there has not *been* a defined market to fit into. In the last half of the twentieth century, this market consisted of just a few names—Arturo Islas, Reinaldo Arenas, Michael Nava, and Francisco X. Alarcon, among others—and very few anthologies of their works, which Charles Rice-González notes in his introduction to the 2011 collection *From Macho to Mariposa: New Gay Latino Fiction* (vii). Furthermore, unlike their Chicana feminist counterparts, these authors were never really organized in any substantial way, meaning that there was little established audience eager to purchase their books, certainly an enticement for publishing houses in picking up new authors in the genre.

Nevertheless, much of this has changed in recent years, thanks to the internet. Readers no longer have to depend on publishers to group works together in order for them to be "found," given that the internet has offered unprecedented opportunities to both readers and authors to do that work themselves. Readers can now easily find books that suit their tastes instead of being limited to the selections that bookstores carry. Authors meanwhile are able to sell books to those whom they might not have been able to reach before the rise of Amazon or like websites. Many of these works, particularly the ones published by university and smaller presses (such as González's) are not likely carried by large bookstores, or are not carried for long periods of time if they do not sell well. On Amazon, however, buying literature is a much more reader-focused process—almost everything is available through a simple search, and most books are rarely out of stock or print. Even if they are, surely somebody is selling a used copy (also listed on Amazon), and if one needs a copy right away, many titles are available for immediate download to an e-reader, which is how I obtained *Still Water Saints*. In short, online book retailers have brought consumers closer to the authors they may want to read, and authors closer to the readers they previously may not have had access to.

What is impressive about Amazon is the sheer number of consumer-driven features the website promotes, allowing readers to add their own unique configuration of commodification independent of the influence of publishing houses.[12] A quick visit to the listing of any book on the website may lead a consumer to other works listed in sidebars such as "Frequently Bought Together" and "Customers Who Bought This Item Also Bought." While the ultimate goal for Amazon is to sell more books, something that Anderson of *Wired* magazine has termed the "Long Tail,"[13] these features also offer keen insights into how readers make communities among themselves by organizing authors of interest. On the homepage of the author, we also see another feature that is directed by consumer—"Customers Also Bought Items By," followed by a list of additional authors. There are several other features I have not mentioned here, including sales rankings, publication information, and importantly, reader reviews. A 2006 study by Chevalier and Mayzlin indicates that readers frequently do take these into account when deciding to purchase a book,[14] and here we may see the importance of a website such as goodreads.com, which is review oriented.

---

12. I use the example of Amazon because it is the 500-pound gorilla in the market, but other retailers do employ almost identical features.

13. According to Anderson, a few popular products still account for a large number of overall sales on Amazon, but in their aggregate, sales of more obscure items or of books that Amazon carries but Barnes and Noble stores do not rival the few at the top. As Anderson explains, "the average Barnes & Noble carries 130,000 titles. Yet more than half of Amazon's book sales come from *outside* its top 130,000 titles. Consider the implication: If the Amazon statistics are any guide, the market for books that are not even sold in the average bookstore is larger than the market for those that are." Recommendations, Anderson writes, serve to drive demand "down the Long Tail." Using the example of subscription music service Rhapsody, a user who clicks on Britney Spears, pop superstar, is recommended Pink, a pop-rock musician who has never reached Spears's level of fame. From Pink's page there is a recommendation for 1980s ska band The Selecter, so "in three clicks, Rhapsody may have enticed a Britney Spears fan to try an album that can hardly be found in record stores" (Anderson).

14. In their study of over 1,600 titles, the authors find that customer reviews tend to be positive on both Amazon's and Barnes and Noble's websites but are more detailed at Amazon (354). Interestingly, they also note that "the relatively rare one-star reviews carry a lot of weight with consumers"; they attribute this to the possibility that consumers believe that five-star reviews may come from authors themselves looking to hype their works, while a one-star review would be more likely to come from somebody who has actually read the book (349–50). When purchasing consumer products on Amazon, I tend to give far more

As we saw in the cases of Muñoz and Espinoza, their publishers seem to almost purposefully avoid mentioning that they are gay authors, or that many of their stories heavily feature queer plots and characters. Aside from readers who inadvertently come across this surprising content, as demonstrated in the goodreads.com review left by Salem seen earlier, avoidance of queerness also misses readers who may expressly purchase these works *because* of this content. Amazon's features work to negate this avoidance—looking to drive sales down the Long Tail, it shows consumers how other readers have connected works and suggests that they do the same. As a result, readers are able to discover other authors that may be of interest to them, putting together audience-composed genres that may not have otherwise existed. Over the course of writing *Capturing Mariposas*, I tracked changes in the list of authors featured on the pages for Espinoza, González, and Muñoz in Amazon's "Customers Also Bought Items By" feature. Although these three authors have not appeared in any collections together, nor are they printed by the same publishing houses, they have had a substantial degree of connectivity at various times. They are also strongly connected to other queer Latinx authors such as Justin Torres, Gloria Anzaldúa, and Benjamin Alire Sáenz, among a host of other names.

CONCLUSION

Of course, such a study is also fraught with weaknesses, which is why I did not include the full version of it here. Keen, for example, warns that marketplace data should be treated carefully because "one can never know for sure if a person who purchases a text, for education or for pleasure, actually takes the step of becoming one of its real readers" (*Narrative* 34). In short, we cannot know with certainty if those who are buying particular books are reading them, if those reading them are students forced to buy them for a class, or if they are given away as gifts. We also have no insight into actual sales figures driven

---

weight to one-star reviews so as to have an indication of potential problems with the product in question, as opposed to five-star reviews, which tend to be almost gushing and not very informative.

by Amazon, nor into the algorithms they use to determine movement on these connectivity lists. What these lists do suggest is that readers have real power to intervene in the book market and support nascent genres such as that of gay Chicano literature, even if they may not be aware they are doing so. As we have seen, this helps to negate some of the power of publishing houses that have commodified these works to fit into an already defined market, hopefully landing these books in the hands of sympathetic/empathetic readers who will consider, and even act upon, their unique and substantial political potential.

CHAPTER 5

Conversations with the Authors

WHEN I INITIALLY set out on this project, I specifically chose to work with Espinoza, González, and Muñoz not only because they represent a generational cohort having emerged around the same time but also because their works are enjoyable on a visceral level and not enough academic work has been done with them. This last point is particularly surprisingly in an author like Muñoz, who accomplishes fascinating things in terms of form throughout all of his works—by all rights, he should be a star subject in the field of narratology, and Martínez and Moya have both rightfully picked up on that, as I discussed in chapter 2. To put a natural cap to this book and add to the academic conversation, speaking to them was imperative in order to capture their views of many of the subjects I highlight throughout this work: writing as a minority (gay) within a minority (Chicanx), their path to becoming published authors, and audience reaction to their works, among other areas. In early 2015, I had the opportunity to speak with both Espinoza and Muñoz, and although González was unavailable, here I also include from his substantial online interview archive. While this chapter could not possibly encapsulate everything that they shared, it does, I believe, bring this project to its natural conclusion. Although they all have experienced great successes, the path has not always been smooth, and those road bumps have sometimes come from surprising directions.

STILL WATER STARTING POINTS

The genesis of all three authors' first works came through professional writing programs, where they now make their own careers. Nevertheless, as Espinoza explained, it was never his intention to produce a novel: "I was deathly afraid of that word, *novel*. To write something in small chunks just because I'm a big slacker and I didn't want to think that way." Encouraged by author and professor Susan Straight, he enrolled in an advanced writing course, where he decided to write stories focused on a botánica near his mother's house. As he explained: "One of the things I loved so much about the shops were the eclecticism, how you could find all of these different religious images and iconographies in a shop sandwiched between a nail salon and a donut store in a very sort of mundane strip mall." He cited Laura Esquivel's *Like Water for Chocolate,* which he was reading at the time, as another strong influence on his writing process, but inspiration also came from another surprising source: working in retail as an assistant manager at Hot Topic. As he recalled: "I worked retail for many years and what always fascinated me when I worked at a store were those moments of quiet when everything had settled, the lights were off . . . how it just comes to a crashing halt. The way in which you can trace the echoes and the memories and the voices of the people who have come and gone through those spaces." As I mentioned in chapter 3, the focus on the mundanities of the retail world in *Still Water Saints* may work to demystify the botánica, for many a site that drips of the rhetoric of magic realism.

Despite the ultimate way that the novel appears to have been marketed, Espinoza did not see it as having anything to do with magic realism. He explained, "What I wanted to capture with Perla was the fact that she's not someone who's magical and this isn't about magical realism. The thing that makes these people who own the botánicas so special is the skill they have at listening. That was what I tried to capture more than anything." He further explained that his goal was not to produce another version of Anaya's *Bless Me, Ultima* because it "had already been done and also because I wanted to combat that notion.... We're not all about flying pigs and rivers rolling backwards and spirits." Instead, he wanted to focus on the importance of faith in folk remedies that he had grown up with, even if "we never fully believed that they worked." He explained: "[As kids] we took a pill, but my mother would also use these kooky remedies.... [T]here isn't magic, but there's this faith and belief in what you're doing.... [It's] the exploration of culture and the way culture is embedded in our DNA and it's hard to shake." He considered this cultural realism in the face of the magical as integral to *Still Water Saints*: "I want to look at these echoes of the past, of our culture that often times we think that we're no longer under their influence but in reality we still are. They still leave traces. So the reason why I started with 'She could walk on water,' precisely my aim was to build this expectation and then completely fuck with it."

Nevertheless, toying with a genre so connected to Latin America is bound to bring comparisons to its authors, which Martín-Rodríguez explores in his *Life in Search of Readers*. For Espinoza, this is not only highly problematic but downright insulting in many cases. As he explained:

> I think that my problem a lot of the time about publishing and writers of color is that they have a tendency to exalt someone to a certain level to the detriment of everyone else. So you'll get comments like, "You write just like Sandra Cisneros, or you write just like Gabriel García Márquez." Somebody told me that in an interview and I thought, "Where are you getting that?" You're a Mexican American writer and your story reminded me of—have you read Junot Díaz? I don't go up to WASP writers and say, "So much of your writing reminds me of John Updike," or "Have you read Ernest Hemmingway?" You just don't do that. You get a lot of that rhetoric, unfortunately, and it's very frustrating.

TRANSITIONING TO *DIEGO*

In chapter 3, I discussed how it may be easier for a Latinx author to be published if they are producing what the market expects—namely, works that somehow fit into the magical-realist tradition. We may see that as the case in *Still Water Saints*, which, at least superficially, connects to that tradition fairly well. While Espinoza did not talk about the behind-the-scenes of that novel, he did talk extensively about his second, *The Five Acts of Diego León*, which has strong parallels to the early life of actor Ramón Novarro. Although I have only mentioned that work tangentially in chapter 4, it is centered upon a well-off young Mexican man who, during the postrevolutionary strife that raged on in parts of the country, decides to pursue his dreams of acting in Hollywood. After struggling, he manages to become quite successful until the advent of talkies, at which point he becomes unmarketable due to his thick accent. Interlaced with this story is the protagonist's coming to terms with his own sexuality, and although he never "comes out of the closet," he does have a baby with a lesbian costar, Fiona, who advises him on the pitfalls of being a closeted actor.

Writing *Diego León* as gay was not his original intention, as Espinoza explained in the interview. While describing the work to a peer, he recalled that "she looked at me and said matter-of-factly, 'Well, he's gay, right?' And it was this moment, I stopped and said, 'Well, I guess he is.' That was the missing ingredient in a lot of the early versions of Diego and his earlier manifestations." Given that it is also a historical work, Espinoza said that he "agonized" over getting the details right: "It's hard because you introduce that factor into the writing when you're worried about plot and setting, point of view and the structure. And suddenly you have to worry about, well, what kind of pants were they wearing? What are spats? It makes it even harder." Certainly, this was not a consideration in his earlier *Still Water Saints*, which occurs in the present day and in a setting with which Espinoza is highly familiar. In *Diego León* we see these two complications that were not present in the earlier work—an earlier setting in postrevolutionary Mexico that may not be recognizable to an American audience, and the gay factor that played a very minor role in *Still Water Saints*.

While Espinoza did not specify if these factors were problematic for the publisher, he did say that they initially "really liked the book"—indeed, they bought it and *Still Water Saints* as a package. Nevertheless, he added: "That was my task, but it was a very different book." Candidly, Espinoza talked about behind-the-scenes changes that affected the final product, including losing his original editor to a promotion, then losing a second to another publishing house, creating an unstable working environment. Espinoza recalled that the book originally had much material that was jettisoned—"I had a journal excerpt from the reporter that [Diego] meets on the train. His observations of what he's seeing, the Mexican people. I had bus tickets, pages of scripts, I had all of this crazy stuff going on." The publisher felt that this was perhaps too experimental, and, as Espinoza noted, "a big publishing house like Random House doesn't really do experimental unless you're someone like Jennifer Egan." Summing up Random House's reaction, Espinoza said that "in a lot of ways, they just didn't know what to do with it" given that it did not follow Latinx author tropes of "poor immigrant stories, where we're crossing the border and we're being chased by the border patrol and we're hopelessly poor. Or the gang member story, or the magical realism story." Nevertheless, he said that he still stands by it and "still is proud of it and a lot of the writing in it." From a reader perspective, the book is not as cohesive as I had hoped that it would be, but speaking critically, it is well worth inquiry given the very different subject areas that it tackles.

MUÑOZ ZAGS

Muñoz, meanwhile, spoke extensively about the difficulties he had in finding a publisher for his first collection, *Zigzagger*. He recounted that "nobody" was taking the book originally, which is why he turned to work on *The Faith Healer of Olive Avenue,* which would turn out to be a more traditional collection. He said that much of the reaction to *Zigzagger* could be summed up as "we're not sure if Chicano lit is ready for this kind of material. I guess they meant queer narrative, but I guess the other thing I didn't anticipate was there was such a sense of experimentation," a facet I discussed in depth in chapter 2. Muñoz said he understands why readers may see that collection as experimental, that "most people teach the first book and not the second because there's so much more to think about with form," even though he did not necessarily agree with the assessment. It was suggested that the problem with *Zigzagger* may be in the arrangement of the stories, which I also discussed in chapter 2—it begins by destabilizing the reader, but is not strongly queer until later in the collection. Ultimately, it was through connections with author peers Rick Yañez and Rigoberto González that he got the attention of Ilan Stavans and his Latino Voices series at Northwestern University, which is where that collection ended up. Later, *Faith Healer* went to Algonquin Press, along with his first novel, *What You See in the Dark*.

Many times, Muñoz's hallmark of toying with the narrator role boils down to a technique he calls witnessing by inference or suggestion. Speaking specifically about "Lindo y Quierdo," the first story of *Faith Healer*, he explained that it "lets the reader know that a motorcycle accident has occurred, but we're not actually at the scene. The mother certainly isn't at the scene, and when she dwells on the moment, she has to go back to one of her own experiences in a car accident to generate the feeling of the trauma that her son must have experienced right at the time." He further explains that when characters or readers fill these blanks, "it's an act of imagination. And that, to me, is very powerful. Where people's minds will force them to go when the facts are not there. And I think that we do that as a matter of course in our own lives. Particularly with trauma. Particularly when we hear the pain of others in our families." Another narrator that I explored in the case of Muñoz—the confrontational—had its genesis in the story "The Unimportant Lila Parr" being rejected because the magazine that he submitted it to did not publish "gay fiction." He explained:

> It really surprised me because ["Lila Parr"] is about the father—the only queer character in there is a corpse whose story is imagined but

not the entire center of the story. I flew into a rage. I was really upset by the dismissal. Not by the rejection . . . but the dismissal and the categorization of a story that I wasn't quite ready to call just "gay." Or just "queer." So, I said, well, fuck you, you want a gay story, I'll write a gay story.

The result of that rejection was "Monkey Sí," perhaps the most abrasive story that Muñoz has produced. As he recalled, an editor at Boston Review even asked him to tone down the narrator because that role had become too "bruising" toward the reader, which led to scrapping at least one line of the story that perhaps pushed the reader too far. He recalled, laughing: "There's a line in there where the narrator invites a soundtrack and makes fun of Elton John and then someone else and then says the soundtrack should be Lola Beltrán and Amalia Mendoza. When I [originally] submitted that story there was one parenthetical phrase at the end of that—'and fuck you if you don't know who they are.'"

GONZÁLEZ'S INNER WORLD

As evidenced in his substantial archive, the genesis of many of González's works has come from his own life; indeed, he has written several autobiographical works, including *Butterfly Boy* and *An Autobiography of My Hungers*. The troubled father/son relationship has been particularly productive—he told Montgomery that "just when I think I have something sorted out, I become a few years older and I need to mine that material all over again, which is why I keep going back to [that]—I am now on book four!" He revealed to Segura that crossing the border is what initially sparked his creativity—"I looked at a sign on the street and wondered what it meant. My lifelong relationship to poetry began when my English tutor said to me "Here, look at this: PAT PET PIT POT PUT. Every single one of those sounds is a word. The desire to possess these tools—meaning and sound—have only continued to grow." It was a creative writing class in college that encouraged him further—he recounted to *PEN America* that, after reading works by Latinx authors "who wrote about family and Mexico and going to school," he realized that somebody like himself could also be a writer, that "what I experienced and imagine could be interesting enough to be published" (Cerand). He cited Tomás Rivera's *Y no se lo tragó la tierra* as a particular influence that led him to explore his own family's journey as migrant workers in Southern California, which ultimately led to *Crossing Vines* (Gómez), explored here in depth in chapter 1. Although he has long resided in New York City, he is continually pulled back to Mexico and the Southwest, particularly the fictional Caliente Valley where many of his works are set (Segura). For him, the act of writing has also become one of remembrance; given that many of his family members have passed away, including both of his parents (Herbert), his tendency toward autobiography seems to be a way to not only record his own life experiences but also memorialize those who too often fall into the forgotten cracks of history.

STRADDLING TWO WORLDS

As I discussed in chapter 4, getting a book published is only half the battle—it does not guarantee that anybody will buy it, or that it will be read or noticed by reviewers. That seems to have been a major stumbling block for Espinoza's *Diego León,* although the author did recall that "the Historical Review, this organization that reviews historical books, gave me a really great review. They said the details are great, so I was like 'Yes!'" Muñoz spoke far more in depth about a lack of reviews, particularly for *What You See in the Dark,* which he saw as a problem for Latinx authors in general. During the year of its release, according to the VIDA count, "there was something like 760 books reviews in the *New York Times* across all fields. Eight of them were by Latinos." Nevertheless, even in the face of institutional bias against Latinx authors, the sting of not being reviewed is still strong. As Muñoz succinctly put it, "[*What You See in the Dark*] didn't get reviewed, and that kind of sucks." He further elaborated: "We've been fighting all this time to have access to the big literary houses, and I had two books with Algonquin and we could not get any of the major papers to take a look at them."

It could be hoped that, being gay authors, they would be supported by the queer literary scene in ways that the mainstream does not. Unfortunately, that has not occurred, a situation reminiscent of the struggle between Chicana feminists and their Euro-American counterparts that had a strong role in the genesis of their movement. As Muñoz explained:

> *Faith Healer* took a little while to get reviewed. Strangely, it got nominated for an award, for the Lambda, but I never even cite that in my CV. I don't. I apologize to people in my community who won one, but the award means nothing to me. And I wouldn't care if I got nominated or won it or not. When *What You See in the Dark* came out . . . we sent the book out and had it not been for a friend of mine from New York who knew a couple of people really closely, who finally just said what is it going to take? This guy has won a Whiting, he's got an NEA, he's got two books, you nominated him before, and you can't immediately review him within a month or two? I would monitor the site and see books from smaller presses being considered pretty quickly, meaning a month or two or three. It took a year before they reviewed *What You See*. And it happened, I think, because my friend pipped up to a couple of people he knew and said do you realize how fucked up this looks? We can't be talking about what Lambda needs to do in terms of inclusion when you're not even supporting one who is already three books in.

Muñoz took particular umbrage that the community fails to support Rigoberto González, given that he has published well over a dozen books: "The moment that next book comes out, it's the lead thing and championed as someone who's a major part of the community that they're trying to reach out to." Muñoz also mentioned that Espinoza has failed to garner any attention from the white queer publishing world, which is something Espinoza himself did not understand. He explains that Lambda received several copies of *Diego León*, "and they looked at it and scratched their heads and put it aside. " He elaborated: "I'm still not embraced by them and I don't know why. It seems like a lot of times . . . I have to flaunt my Mexicanness more.

Maybe I have to flaunt my gayness more." He continued: "Gay, been with my partner for fifteen years. Fifteen years. I have all of these gay characters in my first book and my second and they're still like, okay. They just look at me."

Straddling the line between queer and Latino has been difficult for these authors, but also productive. For Muñoz, that has manifested itself in the coming-out story, which he returns to many times in his short-story collections. He explained that the genesis of *Zigzagger* came as a "response to some of the things that I was seeing in the late 1990s and early 2000s when I was following queer writers, gay men, in terms of what they were saying in interviews and things like that. And more than once . . . I kept seeing references or a negation of the coming-out story, which really pissed me off." He elaborated that the "white community has advanced, progressed, gotten past the need for coming-out narratives, but those are absent in my community. To see one faction of queer lit saying, okay, we're done, we're over that, we need to move on to something else, was really alienating." That was not Muñoz's experience, growing up in "a small town with extraordinarily conservative values" where they have not yet moved past "that moment of coming out," allowing its authors to write in a "much more joyous and liberated way." As he explained, this need still persists—"this is now 2015, but an 'it gets better video' is not what we need. It's a good encouragement" but not realistic "when it comes down to the reality of living in a small town." Indeed, speaking in relation to this negation and the lack of support from the queer white literary community, Muñoz explained that he does not associate with the term *queer* because "I made the mistake of assuming that the queer community was going to be open to me and my experience, and that wasn't the case. That's why, when people ask me to identify as a queer man or a gay man I'm a little resistant because the word *queer* still has white basically in parenthesis right in front of it." He believed this to be particularly true in the literary community, explaining that "I never felt that my work was considered in the same way that it was with Chicano lit."

González, for his part, seems to express far less conflict between these two worlds. In 2015, he was the recipient of the Lifetime Achievement Award from the Association of Lesbian and Gay Men in Publishing, at which time he told Luongo that "so many of the previous recipients have nurtured and helped me, with my identity as a gay man and as a writer, so joining their company is an absolute honor." González is also based in New York City, the center of the publishing world, and has a long history of service to the profession, including sitting as a board member for the Association of Writers and Writing Programs and the National Book Critics Circle, offering literary criticism for both the *Los Angeles Times* and *El Paso Times* and writing a monthly column for *NBC Latino,* among many others. He has also won countless fellowships, including ones from the National Endowment for the Arts and the Guggenheim. Simply put, González has made himself *impossible* to set aside and ignore. This is echoed in a response that he gave to Olivas in 2007:

> It's important to be true to one's desires and wants. I've seen people come out feeling cheated or dissatisfied with the treatment or reception of their work, only because they don't realize that the responsibility really falls on them to promote the book, be available for readings and keep the book afloat (that is, visible) as long as they can. It's a lot of work, no matter where one publishes. So before writers set out to find a publisher, they should educate themselves about what they have to do for themselves, and then educate their publisher because, big or small, presses sometimes don't always do what's best for a Chicano/Latino writer. In brief, take control and don't depend on others, not agents, not editors, to do it for you.

Nevertheless, as Muñoz explained, the Chicanx literary community is not the affirmative space that one might assume it would be for these artists. This became particularly evident to him with *What You See in the Dark,* which counts the making of Hitchcock's *Psycho* as one of its primary plot points and features only one primary Latina character. The novel itself was born out of Muñoz's fascination with film and a viewing of *Psycho* during a Hitchcock class he took during his time at Harvard University. As Marion Crane (Janet Leigh) is making her escape from Phoenix by car, Muñoz noticed a sign on the highway that directs her to Gorman. He explained, "She's driving towards the Valley. Here was a narrative that did not say

Central Valley, it didn't say anything about where it was in California, just California 'not Los Angeles,' California 'not San Francisco.' And just by the timing of her drive I thought . . . that story takes place in the Valley." The Central Valley is where Muñoz was born and raised, and is the settling of all of his works. As he explained: "I don't think I'll ever write anything that won't be set or connected to the Valley somehow"; it is a setting he considers largely absent in American literature, with some important exceptions. In terms of how the novel was received, he said: "I'm still trying to work on diplomatically phrasing what some of the reaction has been. They come from my peers. And they've come thirdhand and in a backhanded way." He elaborated:

> It channeled back to me what I was writing about. The question was always: What are you doing writing about Hitchcock? The question was always asked rhetorically, and I kept waiting—well, why don't you hazard an answer? Give me the dignity of any artist who produces something and wants a reaction when he or she can't speak for himself. It's almost implied—you shouldn't be writing about those things. It leaves the work to me. . . . I'm not claiming that I wrote a great book or a good book or a necessary book. Maybe it's a sociological thing. The explaining of a self for any writer of color—what are you doing? Maybe I'm just becoming old enough to realize that I would like other people to answer that question. You're the reader—you're the critic. If it's a book that's not adhering to your definitions, maybe it's the definitions that need to be reassigned, reclaimed, realigned.

This reaction has prompted Muñoz to pull back for his next collection: "I don't want to say that I've retreated to family history, but I think I've been cowed a little bit by how harsh the silence has been. Not only from my own community but also from the whole literary scene." As he further explained:

> Should I retreat a bit and write for the community that I know is going to read it, and read it maybe with a certain narrow set of expectations? Or, do I go the other way and say, well, I want to stretch this

a little bit even though I know the consequences might be that people within my own community are going to say, "What in the fuck are you doing? Could you tone it down a bit and do something different?" It's hard.

While González does not go into specifics, he has also revealed that he does have his critics in both the queer and Chicano communities—"people who have been appalled by my representations of Mexicanos and gay relationships. I knew I wasn't going to make everyone happy, but I'm not here to contribute to the romanticization of immigrants or to the idealization of gay partnerships. I'm here to tell my story" (Olivas).

COMMUNITY, PRESENT AND FUTURE

Despite difficulties that Espinoza and Muñoz have encountered in the literary world, they both take heart in this growing community of gay Chicano authors that has been the basis of this project. For Espinoza, he believed that the connection has been forged by the fact that "so many of us just grew up hiding. We grew up in these hypermasculine cultures, and we grew up hiding, having to mute those things," which also speaks to the importance Muñoz places on the coming-out story. Espinoza also saw the common thread of an interrogation of "the presence of the male persona, structures of masculinity in our work, how we are unraveling that and sometimes contradicting it," and said that his third book will focus on "this whole notion of masculinity in our culture and the way in which, as men of color, the things that we are forced to do with our bodies in order to survive." In regard to the current generation of gay Chicano authors, Espinoza said that "now we have this sort of ticket, this license to be free and open and it's almost like we don't know quite what to do with it yet." Speaking with these authors, I got the general sense that by and large, this is true. These authors have not yet extensively worked together like the Chicana feminists have done over the past several decades, even if they do know each other and are familiar with each other's works. The content of their production may also be seen to lack a certain cohesiveness that one would expect from a genre. As Muñoz explained:

> I don't often think that our books are in conversation with each other, and I wonder what that means. I don't know what it means. Sometimes I wonder if they have to be in conversation with each other and that's really the work of the critics to do that for us. In some way, we're kind of relying on the critics to group us in that way so that there is a power in numbers.

As I have noted throughout this book, critics have been slow to put these authors together, but that too is changing, as we see with the growth of jotería studies.

Both Espinoza and Muñoz were happy that young, queer authors of color are picking up their works, and can see the results of that connection when they visit campuses. Espinoza explained: "Everywhere I go, whenever I speak, one of the things I talk about is growing up in the closet and I'm talking to these huge populations of Latino students, so often they come up to me and say, 'Thank you for saying that. I'm gay, and you suddenly gave me an opportunity to enter into this discussion.'" He continued: "The more of us that write, the more of us that give young Chicano queer writers out there an opportunity to see that it's okay—they're going to feel more comfortable doing it themselves." Muñoz, however, did not see their issues as the same—they are growing up in a different world. He explained: "It's interesting to me that some of them call my work more historical [laughs], like 1980s. And it's true, that is another era. It's not the now, it's not what it means to be queer in 2015. Or for a young Mexicano, somebody who's undocumented." Muñoz believed that the stage is set for transgender work—we clearly see the seeds of this in jotería studies—and he looked forward to the ways in which it will add to and change the conversation.

González believes that "mentorship is a Chicano value" (Olivas). He explained that "people who do not want to participate in these conversations should please cease from making such comments as 'I don't want to be known as a Chicano writer' or 'I don't want to be known as a gay writer.' We need role models, not cowards" (Vazquez).

Muñoz in particular spent a good deal of time talking about this own mentors, and the enormous influence they had on their own work and career. He held particular reverence for Helena Maria Viramontes, author of *Under the Feet of Jesus* and *Their Dogs Came with Them*, along with critical work. For the upcoming generation, he said, "I don't know how I'll be of service to that other than being, I don't want to call it the old guard, but that's essentially how our mentors treated us." He added, referring to his mentors, but with an eye toward those who will come after him: "They made it very clear: We set the stage for you, so work. Do it. Do something."

As we have seen in his *Red-Inked Retablos,* González, known for activism, has taken a critical role in cultivating and organizing the next generation of queer Latinx voices. He explained to Lumpkin that "being an activist-writer means keeping the door open for others, not closing it right behind you. It means asking yourself what you can do, not only who you can be." For him, engaging the growing community of queer Latinx authors is particularly exciting and seems to best encapsulate his approach both as an author and a public figure: "To be part of that community is empowering; to spread the word is life-saving. That's what I call literary activism."

CONCLUSION

Branching Out

NOT UNLIKE Chicanx and Latinx authors in general, gay Chicanos have made great strides in the past few decades in terms of entering the book market and solidifying expressions of their subjectivities in view of the reading public. If we remember that one of the first of these novels, Rechy's *City of Night* (1963), was not accepted into the Chicanx literary canon until some two decades after he became active as a writer, their progress is particularly impressive. Rechy was soon joined by a wave that included names such as Francisco X. Alarcón, Arturo Islas, Michael Nava, and Richard Rodriguez—who produced a variety of works that entered into disparate areas of the market. This included the more explicitly sexual (Rechy), the political (Rodriguez), and even the crime genre, as we see in Nava's Henry Rios series of novels. The wave that has emerged since 2000 has only added to that diversity, and together they speak to a myriad of issues that mark the lives of gay Chicanos: homophobia and a persistent machismo (present in so many of these works), HIV/AIDS (a focus of Gil Cuadros's *City of God* and a disease that cut short Islas's life), and racism and class discrimination—and frequently, the intersection of the two, as we see in Muñoz's "Monkey Sí." In this book, I have written of only a few themes present in these works; there is much more cover.

Aside from the cultural schema that I have looked at throughout this book, one of the aims of *Capturing Mariposas* has been to fill a critical gap to perhaps engender more literary analysis of these works. While the current generation of Jotería scholars have made great strides in establishing a forum to express their subjectivities, as I highlighted in the introduction, their work has not included a substantial amount of literary criticism, and academic treatment of Espinoza, González, and Muñoz, although growing, certainly does not match that of the generation of gay Chicano writers that emerged primarily in the 1980s.[1] I firmly believe that this will come in time. The authors that I talk about in this book have been open about their sexuality and have reproduced multitudes of queer Chicanx lives in their work; the quality of their writing is growing ever stronger, and the quantity is unmatched. González may be the most prolific gay Latino author yet, producing books for children and adolescents, autobiographies, collections of short stories, and poetry, in addition to his recent meditation on Gay Chicano literature, *Red Inked Retablos*. Muñoz has also produced two explicitly gay-themed story collections, *Zigzagger* and *Faith Healer*, while his most recent *What You See* extended beyond categories of gay and Latinx to reach toward a more general-interest reading public. And while Alex Espinoza's *Still Water Saints* largely lacks queer content, his most recent *The Five Acts of Diego Leon* features a gay protagonist. Both Muñoz and Espinoza have new works in the pipelines, while González continues to be an authorial powerhouse, producing eight titles since 2010.

The importance of these authors producing gay Chicano subjectivities in their writing cannot be overstated. Whether fair or not, the criticism that Cherríe Moraga leveled against some in that earlier generation in "Queer Aztlán" was that they were *not* doing this when they should have been. Given the mounting volume of literary

---

1. *Queer in Aztlán* provides an excellent bibliography of these critical works, including the thorough work that Aldama has done with Islas (*Dancing With Ghosts* and *Critical Mappings*), various works by Foster (*El Ambiente Nuestro, Sexual Textualities,* and *Chicano/Latino Homoerotic Identities*), and Bruce-Novoa's 1986 article "Homosexuality and the Chicano novel," among others too numerous to list here.

works, with Espinoza, González, and Muñoz adding ever more, this is why I believe that we can and *should* speak of Gay Chicano literature as a genre unto itself: these authors are forcefully talking about lives that have rarely been represented in any medium and are being noticed for it in their connection with readers. As we saw in chapter 4, the publisher, author, and reader all have distinct roles to play in the formation of genre, but I hold the author-audience relationship as most critical because this is where we can see the political implications of these books. Ultimately, this is why I chose a cognitive/narrative approach in the content chapters—I believe that it really gets at the heart of how we read literature, and what we take away from it in that process. In a critical context, in the introduction I wrote of the internalization that underlies so much of Queer and Jotería Studies, and I believe that the cognitive approach also serves to highlight that relationship.

Nevertheless, this approach is not completely removed from theory, but rather works to complement it. This is why I chose to speak of cultural schema in each chapter—the real-world implications that these texts challenge, reaffirm, and transform through their narrative techniques. In chapter 1, I looked at how González employs empathy and sympathy to construct affective planes that connect characters to readers, challenging cultural schema and leading to cross-understanding that may lead readers to reevaluate their own relationships or misconceptions of groups, such as agricultural workers or gays. Although *Crossing Vines* is not an explicitly queer work, I did include it in order to highlight the emotive techniques that González tends to employ in much of his writing. In chapter 2, I considered how Muñoz constructs the vague narrator—one that forces the reader to employ Theory of Mind to go back and reconstruct missing parts of the text by considering the narrator as a character. With these missing pieces, we see the reaffirmation of cultural schema of a hidden and shameful homosexuality that is prevalent in much early queer Chicanx narrative, and in Chicanx lives and communities. In chapter 3, I looked at how Espinoza uses cognitive surprise to deconstruct the idea of magical realism in *Still Water Saints*, instead transforming the site of the magical—Perla's botánica—into a community-focused location of openness and inclusion where even a transvestite like Azúcar is not judged for merely existing. In the process, he may even shift reader expectations of Latinx literature in general, a genre prone to magic realization by publishers eager to cash in on an established market. In chapter 4, I considered this market distortion, the political implication of these works for the reader, and how the reader is intervening in the market, putting these authors together in ways that publishers have so far not done.

In chapter 5, I decided to let the authors speak for themselves. Critical studies such as these typically do not include this author dimension, but I believe that it is of the utmost importance here given that I want to extend the critical record of these writers. Aside from that, since I have spent a great deal of ink in *Capturing Mariposas* ruminating on what I *think* these authors are doing in their texts, I wanted to get their take on what they intended to instill in their readers. I believe these interviews have not only managed to accomplish that important task but also include critical insights into the difficulties that the authors have encountered in the publishing industry, how they feel being part of this wider genre of Gay Chicano literature, and their rejection from and of mainstream Queer literature, which they see as largely a construct of white queerness. Interestingly, much of what the authors revealed were elements that I had already speculated upon in the content chapters of this book. For example, instead of calling it a vague narrator, Muñoz commented that he writes trauma events from the perspective of witnessing by inference and suggestion. Espinoza confirmed that he did intend to build Perla up as a magical entity, then deconstruct this expectation, reimaging her and the botánica as a site of culture and community. For myself, particularly important were their thoughts on Gay Chicano literature as a genre, and how they have witnessed it evolve throughout their careers.

In its cognitive and narratological approach, *Capturing Mariposas* has aimed to branch off into new pathways about how we look at this genre, focusing on the wave to emerge since 2000, but it has really only scratched the surface. I purposefully overlooked poets here because it is beyond my strengths as a critic, but here we should add names such as Eduardo C. Corral, who has won numerous awards in his thus far short career, Miguel Murphy, and those published in the 2012 tome *Joto: An Anthology of Queer Xicano Poetry*. Benjamin Alire Saénz, who has written an extensive number of books, is another author who deserves mention. He won the prestigious PEN/Faulkner Award for Fiction in 2013 for *Everything Begins and Ends at the Kentucky Country Club*, and is now fully exploring gay Chicano subjectivities in his writing after coming out of the closet in his 50s. Alex Sánchez, who has published eight books since 2001, has been criminally overlooked, perhaps because his works are directed towards queer adolescents, a segment of the market that tends to be a critical blind spot. Toward the end of his *Red Inked Retablos,* González also names many more that have yet to enter into any sort of substantial critical conversation (133–38), and *Queer in Aztlán* provides a substantial bibliography worthy of deep consideration.

As Muñoz noted toward the end of our interview, there are even more gay Chicano writers coming, and they will undoubtedly both work within the framework that these authors have constructed and expand it even further. Recent collections such as *From Macho to Mariposa: New Gay Latino Fiction* showcase many authors that have not been published elsewhere, and although the quality of the stories themselves varies, there is some true talent featured in it that I hope continues to grow. With the framework that authors such as Espinoza, González, and Muñoz, as well as Rechy, Islas, Alarcón, Nava, and those that came before have provided, hopefully they, and those who have yet to set pen to paper or to have been formally published, will continue to oversee the growth of this fascinating genre.

WORKS CITED

Aldama, Frederick Luis. *Brown on Brown: Chicano/a Representations of Gender, Sexuality, and Ethnicity.* U of Texas P, 2005.

——. "Magical Realism." *The Routledge Companion to Latino/a Literature,* edited by Suzanne Bost and Frances R. Aparicio, Routledge, 2013, pp. 334–41.

——. *Postethnic Narrative Criticism: Magicorealism in Oscar "Zeta" Acosta, Ana Castillo, Julie Dash, Hanif Kureishi, and Salman Rushdie.* U of Texas P, 2003.

——. *Spilling the Beans in Chicanolandia.* U of Texas P, 2006.

Almaguer, Tomás. "Chicano Men: A Cartography of Homosexual Identity and Behavior." *The Lesbian and Gay Studies Reader,* edited by Henry Abelove et al., Routledge, 1993, pp. 255–73.

Alvarez, Pablo. "Gil Cuadros' Azt-land: Documenting a Queer Chicano Literary Heritage." *Queer in Aztlán,* edited by Adelaida R. Del Castillo and Gibrán Güido, San Diego State UP, 2014, pp. 293–302.

Anderson, Chris. "The Long Tail." *Wired,* 1 Oct. 2004, www.wired.com/2004/10/tail/.

Anzaldúa, Gloria. *Borderlands/La Frontera.* Aunt Lute, 1988.

——. "To(o) Queer the Writer." *Living Chicana Theory,* edited by Carla Trujillo, Third Woman, 1998, pp. 263–76.

Arguedas, José María. *The Fox from Up Above, and the Fox from Down Below.* Edited by Julio Ortega. Translated by Frances Horning Barraclough. U of Pittsburgh P, 2000.

Arnold, Martin. "Making Books; Many Hispanics, Scant Marketing." *The New York Times,* 21 Mar. 2002. www.nytimes.com/2002/03/21/books/making-books-many-hispanics-scant-marketing.html.

Bal, Mieke. *Narratology: Introduction to the Theory of Narrative.* U of Toronto P, 1997.

Bañalez, Xamuel. "Jotería: A Decolonizing Political Project." *Aztlán,* vol. 39, no. 1, 2014, pp. 155–65.

Baron-Cohen, Simon, Alan M. Leslie, and Uta Firth. "Mechanical, Behavioral and Intentional Understanding of Picture Stories in Autistic Children." *British Journal of Developmental Psychology,* vol. 4, no. 2, pp. 113–25.

Batson, C. Daniel. "These Things Called Empathy: Eight Related but Distinct Phenomena." *The Social Neuroscience of Empathy,* edited by Jean Decety and William Ickes, MIT Press, 2009, pp. 3–15.

Bauman, Zygmunt. *The Intimations of Postmodernity.* Routledge, 1992.

Booth, Wayne C. *The Rhetoric of Fiction.* U of Chicago P, 1961.

Bortolussi, Marisa, and Peter Dixon. *Psychonarratology: Foundations for the Empirical Study of Literary Response.* Cambridge UP, 2003.

Brewer, William F., and Edward H. Lichtenstein. "Stories Are to Entertain: A Structural-Affect Theory of Stories." *Journal of Pragmatics,* vol. 6, 1982, pp. 473–86.

Bruce-Novoa, Juan. "Homosexuality and the Chicano Novel." *Homosexual Themes in Literary Studies,* edited by Wayne R. Dynes and Stephen Donaldson, Garland, 1992, pp. 33–41.

Carroll, Noel. "On Some Affective Relationships between Audiences and the Characters in Popular Fictions." *Empathy: Philosophical and Psychological Perspectives,* edited by Amy Coplan and Peter Goldie, Oxford UP, 2011, pp. 162–84.

Carruthers, Peter. "Autism as Mind-Blindness." *Theories of Theories of Mind,* edited by Peter Carruthers and Peter K. Smith, Cambridge UP, 1996, pp. 257–76.

Cerand, Laura. "The PEN Ten with Rigoberto González." *PEN America,* 3 June 2014, pen.org/the-pen-ten-with-rigoberto-gonzalez/.

Chatman, Seymour. *Coming to Terms: The Rhetoric of Narrative in Fiction and Film.* Cornell UP, 1990.

———. *Reading Narrative Fiction.* Macmillan, 1993.

———. *Story and Discourse: Narrative Structure in Fiction and Film.* Cornell UP, 1978.

Chevalier, Judith A., and Dina Mayzlin. "The Effect of Word of Mouth on Sales: Online Book Reviews." *Journal of Marketing Research,* vol. 43, no. 3, 2006, pp. 345–54.

Clark, Candice. *Misery and Company: Sympathy in Everyday Life.* U of Chicago P, 1997.

———. "Sympathy Biography and Sympathy Margin." *American Journal of Sociology*, vol. 93, no. 2, 1987, pp. 290–321.

Cornejo Polar, Antonio. "*Mestizaje*, Transculturation, Heterogeneity." *The Latin American Cultural Studies Reader*, edited by Ana Del Sarto et al., translated by Christopher Dennis, Duke UP, 2004, pp. 116–19.

Cosmides, Leda, and John Tooby. "Consider the Source: The Evolution of Adaptations for Decoupling and Metarepresentation." *Metarepresentations: A Multidisciplinary Approach*, edited by Dan Sperber, Oxford UP, 2000, pp. 53–115.

Cotera, Marta. "Among the Feminists: Racist Classist Issues—1976." *Chicana Feminist Thought: The Basic Historical Writings*, edited by Alma M. García, Routledge, 1997, pp. 213–20.

Danielson, Marivel T. *Homecoming Queers: Desire and Difference in Chicana Latina Cultural Production*. Rutgers UP, 2009.

Deborah. Comment on *Still Water Saints*. GoodReads.com, 27 Sep. 2007, www.goodreads.com/review/show/6156186.

Decety, Jean, and Thierry Chaminade. "Neural Correlates of Feeling Sympathy." *Neuropsychologia*, vol. 41, 2003, pp. 127–38.

Decety, Jean, and Kalina J. Michalska. "Neurodevelopmental Changes in the Circuits Underlying Empathy and Sympathy from Childhood to Adulthood." *Developmental Science*, vol. 13, no. 6, 2010, pp. 886–99.

Del Castillo, Adelaida R., and Gibrán Güido, editors. *Queer in Aztlán*. San Diego State UP, 2014.

de Vignemont, Frédérique. "When Do We Empathize?" *Empathy and Fairness*, edited by Greg Bock and Jamie Goode, Wiley, 2007, pp. 181–89.

Eisenberg, Nancy, and Natalie D. Eggum. "Empathetic Responding: Sympathy and Personal Distress." *The Social Neuroscience of Empathy*, edited by Jean Decety and William Ickes, MIT Press, 2009, pp. 71–84.

Eisenberg, Nancy, et al. "Empathy-Related Responding: Moral, Social, and Socialization Correlates." *The Social Psychology of Good and Evil: Understanding Our Capacity for Kindness and Cruelty*, edited by A. G. Miller, Guilford, 2004, pp. 386–415.

———. "Prosocial Development." *Handbook of Child Psychology Volume 3: Social, Emotional, Personality Development*, edited by Nancy Eisenberg et al., Hoboken: Wiley, 2006, pp. 646–718.

Esmeralda. Comment on *The Five Acts of Diego León*. Goodreads.com, 14 Aug. 2013, www.goodreads.com/review/show/695058905.

Espinoza, Alex. *The Five Acts of Diego León*. Random House, 2013.

———. *Still Water Saints*. Random House, 2008.

Fish, Stanley. *Is There a Text in This Class? The Authority of Interpretive Communities*. Harvard UP, 1980.

Fludernik, Monika. "The Category of 'Person' in Fiction: *You* and *We* Narrative-Multiplicity and Intermediacy and Indeterminacy of Reference." *Current Trends in Narratology*, edited by Greta Olson, Walter de Gruyter Gmb & Co. KG, 2011, pp. 101–41.

Foster, David William, editor. *Chicano/Latino Homoerotic Identities*. Garland, 1999.

———, editor. *El ambiente nuestro: Chicano/Latino Homoerotic Writing*. Bilingual, 2006.

———, editor. *Sexual Textualities*. U of Texas P, 1997.

Funk, Jeanne B., Heidi Bechtoldt Baldacci, Tracie Pasold, and Jennifer Baumgardner. "Violence Exposure in Real-Life, Video Games, Movies, and the Internet: Is There Desensitization?" *Journal of Adolescence*, vol. 27, 2004, pp. 23–39.

Gallese, Vittorio. "Embodied Simulation: From Mirror Neuron Systems to Interpersonal Relations." *Empathy and Fairness*, edited by Greg Bock and Jamie Goode, Wiley, 2007, pp. 3–11.

Galloway-Thomas, Carolyn. *Empathy in the Global World: An Intercultural Perspective*. Sage, 2010.

García Landa, José Ángel. "Overhearing Narrative." *The Dynamics of Narrative Form*, edited by John Pier, Walter de Gruyter GmbH & Co., 2004, pp. 191–214.

Genette, Gérard. *Narrative Discourse Revisited*. Translated by Jane E. Lewin. Cornell UP, 1990.

Goldie, Peter. "Anti-Empathy." *Empathy: Philosophical and Psychological Perspectives*, edited by Amy Coplan and Peter Goldie, Oxford UP, 2011, pp. 302–17.

Goldman, Corrie. "This Is Your brain on Jane Austen, and Stanford Researchers Are Taking Notes." *The Stanford Report*, 7 Sept. 2012, news.stanford.edu/news/2012/september/austen-reading-fmri-090712.html.

Gómez, Catalina. "Rigoberto González." *The Library of Congress*, 10 Apr. 2014, www.loc.gov/poetry/hispanic-writers/rigoberto-gonzalez.html.

González, Rigoberto. *Butterfly Boy*. U of Wisconsin P, 2006.

———. *Crossing Vines*. U of Oklahoma P, 2003.

———. *Red-Inked Retablos*. U of Arizona P, 2013.

Guerrero, Elisabeth. "The Emperor's New Clothes: Rosa Beltrán's 'La corte de los ilusos.'" *Chasqui*, vol. 31, no. 2, 2002, pp. 3–14.

Hames-García, Michael. "Jotería Studies, or the Political Is Personal." *Aztlán*, vol. 39, no. 1, 2014, pp. 135–41.

Hames-García, Michael, and Ernesto Javier Martínez. "Introduction: Re-Membering Gay Latino Studies." *Gay Latino Studies*, edited by Michael Hames-García and Ernesto Javier Martínez, Duke UP, 2011, pp. 1–18.

Herbert, Jenna. "An Interview with Rigoberto González." *English Blog The College of Saint Rose*, 7 Oct. 2013, https://stroseenglish.wordpress.com/2013/10/07/an-interview-with-rigoberto-gonzalez/.

Hernández, Ellie D. *Postnationalism in Chicana/o Literature and Culture*. U Texas P, 2009.

Hoeken, Hans, and Mario van Vliet. "Suspense, Curiosity, and Surprise: How Discourse Structure Influences the Affective and Cognitive Processing of a Story." *Poetics*, vol. 26, 2000, pp. 277–86.

Hoffman, Martin L. "Empathy: Justice and Moral Judgment." *Empathy and Its Development*, edited by Nancy Eisenberg and Janet Strayer, Cambridge UP, 1987, pp. 47–80.

Hogan, Patrick Colm. *Cognitive Science, Literature, and the Arts: A Guide for Humanists*. Routledge, 2003.

Iran-Nejad, Asghar. "Cognitive and Affective Causes of Interest and Liking." *Journal of Educational Psychology*, vol. 79, no. 2, 1987, pp. 120–30.

Iser, Wolfgang. *The Act of Reading: A Theory of Aesthetic Response*. Johns Hopkins UP, 1978.

———. *The Implied Reader: Patterns of Communication in Prose Fiction from Bunyan to Beckett*. Johns Hopkins UP, 1974.

———. "The Reading Process: A Phenomenological Approach." *Reader Response Criticism*, edited by Jane P. Tompkins, Johns Hopkins UP, 1980, pp. 50–69.

Kagan, Jerome. *Surprise, Uncertainty and Mental Structures*. Harvard UP, 2002.

Kanellos, Nicolás. *Hispanic Immigrant Literature: El sueño del retorno*. U of Texas P, 2011.

Keen, Suzanne. *Empathy and the Novel*. Oxford UP, 2007.

———. "Narrative Empathy." *Toward a Cognitive Theory of Narrative Acts*, edited by Frederick Luis Aldama, U of Texas P, 2010, pp. 61–94.

———. *Narrative Form*. Palgrave MacMillan, 2003.

Kim, Sue J. "Anger, Temporality, and the Politics of Reading *The Woman Warrior*." *Analyzing World Fiction*, edited by Frederick Luis Aldama, U of Texas P, 2011, pp. 93–108.

Kintsch, Walter. "Learning from Text, Levels of Comprehension, or: Why Anyone Would Read a Story Anyway." *Poetics*, vol. 9, 1980, pp. 87–99.

Kreuzbauer, Robert, and Alan J. Malter. "Embodied Cognition and New Product Design: Changing Product Form to Influence Brand Categorization." *Journal of Product Innovation Management*, vol. 22, no. 2, 2005, pp. 165–76.

La Fountain-Stokes, Lawrence. "Gay Shame, Latina- and Latino-Style: A Critique of White Queer Performativity." *Gay Latino Studies*, edited by Michael Hames-García and Ernesto Javier Martínez, Duke UP, 2011, pp. 55–80.

Lamm, Claus, Jean Decety, and Tania Singer. "Meta-Analytic Evidence for Common and Distinct Neural Networks Associated with Directly Experienced Pain and Empathy for Pain." *NeuroImage*, vol. 54, 2011, pp. 2459–502.

Lee, Allyssa. "Still Water Saints." *Entertainment Weekly,* 26 Jan. 2007, ew.com/article/2007/01/26/still-water-saints/.

Leudar, Ivan, and Alan Costall. Introduction. *Against Theory of Mind,* edited by Ivan Leudar and Alan Costall, Palgrave Macmillan, 2009, pp. 1–16.

Leverage, Paula, Howard Mancing, Richard Schweickert, and Jennifer Marston William. Introduction. *Theory of Mind in Literature,* edited by Paula Leverage et al. Purdue UP, 2011, pp. 1–11.

Lorini, Emiliano, and Cristiano Castelfranchi. "The Cognitive Structure of Surprise: Looking for Basic Principles." *Institute of Cognitive Sciences and Technologies*-CNR, 2009, pp. 1–30, https://pdfs.semanticscholar.org/5b9d/bebb4adbd937e289516fe0092da328b2fd6d.pdf.

Lumpkin, Bernard. "Rigoberto González: Populating the Bookshelves." *LAMBDA Literary,* 4 May 2013, www.lambdaliterary.org/interviews/05/04/rigoberto-gonzalez-populating-the-bookshelves/.

Luongo, Michael. "Diversity Celebrated at Publishing Triangle Awards." *Gay City News,* 29 Apr. 2015, gaycitynews.nyc/diversity-celebrated-publishing-triangle-awards/.

Mandolin. Comment on *Still Water Saints.* Goodreads.com, 16 Jun. 2007, www.goodreads.com/review/show/2024011.

Manrique, Jaime. *Eminent Maricones.* U of Wisconsin P, 1999.

Marshall, David. *The Surprising Effects of Sympathy.* U of Chicago P, 1988.

Martínez, Ernesto. *On Making Sense: Queer Race Narratives of Intelligibility.* Stanford UP, 2013.

———. "Shifting the Site of Queer Enunciation: Manuel Muñoz and the Politics of Form." *Gay Latino Studies,* edited by Michael Hames-García and Ernesto Javier Martínez, Duke UP, 2011, pp. 226–49.

Martín-Rodríguez, Manuel M. *Life in Search of Readers: Reading (in) Chicano/a Literature.* U of New Mexico P, 2003.

Matravers, Derek. "Empathy as a Route to Knowledge." *Empathy: Philosophical and Psychological Perspectives,* edited by Amy Coplan and Peter Goldie, Oxford UP, 2011, pp. 19–30.

McCracken, Ellen. "The Postmodern Continuum of Canon and Kitsch: Narrative and Semiotic Strategies of Chicana High Culture and Chica Lit." *Analyzing World Fiction,* edited by Frederick Luis Aldama, U of Texas P, 2011, pp. 165–81.

———. "Sandra Cisneros' *The House on Mango Street*: Community-Oriented Introspection and the Demystification of Patriarchal Violence." *Breaking Boundaries,* edited by Asunción Horno-Delgado et al., U of Massachusetts P, 1989, pp. 62–71.

Meyer, Wulf-Uwe, Michael Niepel, Udo Rudolph, and Achim Schützwohl. "An Experimental Analysis of Surprise." *Cognition & Emotion,* vol. 5, no. 4, 1991, pp. 295–311.

Meyer, Wulf-Uwe, Rainer Reisenzein, and Achim Schützwohl. "Toward a Process Analysis of Emotions: The Case of Surprise." *Motivation and Emotion*, vol. 21, no. 3, 1997, pp. 251–74.

Miall, David S., and Don Kuiken. "Shifting Perspectives." *New Perspectives on Narrative Perspective*, edited by Willie van Peer and Seymour Chatman, State U of New York P, 2001, pp. 289–301.

Michelon, Pascale, Abraham Z. Snyder, Randy L. Buckner, Mark McAvoy, and Jeffrey M. Zacks. "Neural Correlates of Incongruous Visual Information: An Event-Related fMRI Study." *NeuroImage*, vol. 19, 2003, pp. 1612–26.

Miller, David. "'Are They *My* Poor?': The Problem of Altruism in a World of Strangers." *The Ethics of Altruism*, edited by Jonathan Seglow, Frank Cass, 2004, pp. 106–27.

Mitchell, Peter. *Introduction to Theory of Mind: Children, Autism and Apes*. Arnold, 1997.

Montgomery, Sarah Fawn. "'Nonfiction is the most intimate space": An Interview with Rigoberto González." *Prairie Schooner*, 11 June 2015, prairieschooner.unl.edu/blog/nonfiction-most-intimate-space-interview-rigoberto-gonzalez.

Moraga, Cherríe. "Queer Aztlán: The Re-formation of Chicano Tribe." *Latino/a Thought: Culture, Politics, and Society*, edited by Francisco H. Vásquez and Rodolfo D. Lanham, Rowman & Littlefield, 2003, pp. 258–73.

———. *A Xicana Codex of Changing Consciousness: Writings 2000–2010*. Duke UP, 2011.

Moraga, Cherríe, and Gloria Anzaldúa, editors. *This Bridge Called My Back*. Kitchen Table, 1981.

Morrell, Michael E. *Empathy and Democracy: Feeling, Thinking and Deliberation*. Pennsylvania State UP, 2010.

Moya, Paula. "Dancing with the Devil—When the Devil Is Gay." *Gay Latino Studies*, edited by Michael Hames-García and Ernesto Javier Martínez, Duke UP, 2011, pp. 250–58.

———. *The Social Imperative: Race, Close Reading and Contemporary Literary Criticism*. Stamford UP, 2016.

Muñoz, José Esteban. *Disidentifications: Queers of Color and the Performance of Politics*. U of Minnesota P, 1999.

Muñoz, Manuel. *The Faith Healer of Olive Avenue*. Algonquin, 2007.

———. *What You See in the Dark*. Algonquin, 2011.

———. *Zigzagger*. Northwestern UP, 2003.

Nishida, Hiroko. "A Cognitive Approach to Intercultural Communication Based on Schema Theory." *International Journal of Intercultural Relations*, vol. 23, no. 5, 1999, pp. 753–77.

Nünning, Ansgar. "Unreliable, Compared to What?" *Grenzüberschreitungen: Narratologie Im Komtext/Transcending Boundaries: Narratology in Context,* edited by Walter Grünzweig and Andreas Solbach, Gunter Narr Verlag, 1999, pp. 53-74.

Oatley, Keith. "Theory of Mind and Theories of Mind in Literature." *Theory of Mind in Literature,* edited by Paula Leverage et al., Purdue UP, 2011, pp. 13-26.

Olivas, Daniel. "Interview with Rigoberto González." *La Bloga,* 19 Nov. 2007, labloga.blogspot.com/2007/11/interview-with-rigoberto-gonzlez.html.

Ortony, Andrew, and Derek Partridge. "Surprisingness and Expectation Failure: What's the Difference?" Proceedings of the 10th International Joint Conference on Artificial Intelligence, Milan, 23-28 Aug. 1987. *IJCAI,* www.ijcai.org/Proceedings/87-1/Papers/020.pdf.

Palmer, Alan. *Fictional Minds.* U of Nebraska P, 2004.

Paredes, Raymund A. "Special Feature: The Evolution of Chicano Literature." *MELUS,* vol. 5, no. 2, 1978, pp. 71-110.

Pérez, Daniel Enrique. "Toward a Mariposa Consciousness: Reimagining Queer Chicano and Latino Identities." *Aztlán,* vol. 39, no. 2, 2014, pp. 95-127.

Pérez, Hiram. *A Taste for Brown Bodies: Gay Modernity and Cosmopolitan Desire.* New York UP, 2015.

Pesquera, Beatriz M., and Denise A. Segura. "There Is No Going Back: Chicanas and Feminism." *Chicana Feminist Thought: The Basic Historical Writings,* edited by Alma M. García, Routledge, 1997, pp. 294-309.

Phelan, Jim. *Living to Tell about It: A Rhetoric and Ethics and Character Narration.* Cornell UP, 2005.

———. "Voice, Politics, and Judgments in *Their Eyes Were Watching God*: The Initiation, the Launch and the Debate about Narration." *Analyzing World Fiction,* edited by Frederick Luis Aldama, U of Texas P, 2011, pp. 57-74.

———. "Why Narrators Can Be Focalizers—and Why It Matters." *New Perspectives on Narrative Perspective,* edited by Willie van Peer and Seymour Chatman, State U of New York P, 2001, pp. 51-64.

Porter Brown, Neil. "Echoes of the Central Valley." *Harvard Magazine,* May-June 2011, harvardmagazine.com/2011/05/echoes-of-the-central-valley.

Premack, David, and Guy Woodruff. "Does the Chimpanzee Have a Theory of Mind?" *Behavioral and Brain Sciences,* vol. 4, 1978, pp. 515-26.

Prince, Gerald. "Introduction to the Study of the Narratee." *Reader-Response Criticism: For Formalism to Post-Structuralism,* edited by Jane P. Tompkins, Johns Hopkins UP, 1980, pp. 7-25.

———. "A Point of View on Point of View or Refocusing Focalization." *New Perspectives on Narrative Perspective,* edited by Willie van Peer and Seymour Chatman, State U of New York P, 2001, pp. 43-50.

Rama, Ángel. *Transculturación narrativa en América Latina.* Siglo Veintiuno, 1982.

Ratcliffe, Sophie. *On Sympathy.* Oxford UP, 2008.

Reddy, Vasudevi, and Paul Morris. "Participants Don't Need Theories: Knowing Minds in Engagement." *Against Theory of Mind,* edited by Ivan Leudar and Alan Costall, Palgrave Macmillan, 2009, pp. 91–107.

Reisenzein, Rainer. "The Subjective Experience of Surprise." *The Message Within: The Role of Subjective Experience in Social Cognition and Behavior,* edited by H. Bless, and J. P. Forgas, Psychology, 2000, pp. 262–80.

Renee. Comment on *Butterfly Boy.* Goodreads.com, 9 Dec. 2008, www.goodreads.com/review/show/39752752.

Revilla, Anita Tijerina, and José Manuel Santillana. "Jotería Identity and Consciousness." *Aztlán,* vol. 39, no. 1, 2014, pp. 167–79.

Rice-González, Charles. Introduction from the Editors. *From Macho to Mariposa: New Gay Latino Fiction,* edited by Charles Rice-González and Charlie Vázquez, Tincture, 2011, pp. vii–x.

Richards, Ivor Armstrong. *Practical Criticism.* Routledge, 1964.

Robbins, Jill. "Globalization, Publishing, and the Marketing of 'Hispanic' Identities." *Iberoamericana,* vol. 3, no. 9, 2003, pp. 89–101.

Roberts, Nancy. *Schools of Sympathy: Gender and Identification through the Novel.* McGill-Queen's UP, 1997.

Rockoff, Adam. *Going to Pieces: The Rise and Fall of the Slasher Film, 1978–1986.* McFarland, 2002.

Rodríguez, Juana. *Sexual Futures, Queer Gestures and Other Latina Longings.* New York UP, 2014.

Rodríguez, Richard T. "Carnal Knowledge: Chicano Gay Men and the Dialectics of Being." *Gay Latino Studies,* edited by Michael Hames-García and Ernesto Javier Martínez, Duke UP, 2011, pp. 113–40.

———. *Next of Kin: The Family in Chicano/a Cultural Politics.* Duke UP, 2009.

Salem. Comment on *The Five Acts of Diego León.* Goodreads.com, 31 Jan. 2014, www.goodreads.com/review/show/840255894.

Scheff, Thomas J. *Catharsis in Healing, Ritual, and Drama.* U of California P, 1979. Print.

Schwartz, Barry. *The Paradox of Choice.* HarperCollins, 2004.

Seglow, Jonathan. "Altruism and Freedom." *The Ethics of Altruism,* edited by Jonathan Seglow, Frank Cass, 2004, pp. 145–63.

Segura, Olga. "Poetry, Loss, and Inspiration: An Interview with Rigoberto González." *America: The Jesuit Review,* 5 Aug. 2014, www.americamagazine.org/content/all-things/poetry-loss-and-inspiration-interview-rigoberto-gonzalez.

Shott, Susan. "Emotion and Social Life: A Symbolic Interactionalist Analysis." *American Journal of Sociology,* vol. 84, no. 6, 1979, pp. 1317–34.

Singer, Tania. "The Neuronal Basis of Empathy and Fairness." *Empathy and Fairness*, edited by Greg Bock and Jamie Goode, Wiley, 2007, pp. 20–30.

Singer, Tania, and Claus Lamm. "The Social Neuroscience of Empathy." *The Year in Cognitive Neuroscience 2009*, vol. 1156, no. 1, 2009, pp. 81–96.

Soto, Sandra K. *Reading Chican@ Like a Queer: The Demastry of Desire*. U Texas P, 2010.

Spolsky, Ellen. *Gaps in Nature*. State U of New York P, 1993.

Stanzel, F. K. *A Theory of Narrative*. Translated by Charlotte Goedsche. Cambridge UP, 1984.

Steuber, Karsten R. *Rediscovering Empathy: Agency, Folk Psychology and the Human Sciences*. MIT Press, 2006.

Tan, Ed S. "Emotion, Art, and the Humanities." *Handbook of Emotions*, edited by Michael Lewis and Jeannette M. Haviland-Jones, Guilford, 2000, pp. 116–34.

Tobin, Vera. "Cognitive Bias and the Poetics of Surprise." *Language of Literature*, vol. 18, no. 2, 2009, pp. 155–72.

Tongson, Karen. *Relocations: Queer Suburban Imaginaries*. New York UP, 2011.

Torres, Hector A. *Conversations with Contemporary Chicana and Chicano Writers*. U of New Mexico P, 2007.

Trout, J. D. *The Empathy Gap: Building Bridges to the Good Life and the Good Society*. Viking, 2009.

Urroz, Eloy. "El *crack* en el vórtice de la novela mexicana." *Crack: Instrucciones de uso*, edited by Ricardo Chávez et al., Mondadori, 2004, pp. 149–62.

van Lange, Paul A. M., et al. "A Social Interaction Analysis of Empathy and Fairness." *Fairness*, edited by Greg Bock and Jamie Goode, Wiley, 2007, pp. 97–105.

van Peer, Willie. "Justice in Perspective." *New Perspectives on Narrative Perspective*, edited by Willie van Peer and Seymour Chatman, State U of New York P, 2001, pp. 325–38.

Vazquez, Lauro. "An Interview with Rigoberto González." *Letras Latinas Blog*, 22 Jan. 2012, letraslatinasblog.blogspot.com/2012/01/interview-with-rigoberto-gonzalez.html.

Vermeule, Blakey. *Why Do We Care about Literary Characters?* Johns Hopkins UP, 2010.

Viego, Antonio. "The Place of Gay Male Chicano Literature in Queer Chicano/a Cultural Work." *Gay Latino Studies*, edited by Michael Hames-García and Ernesto Javier Martínez, Duke UP, 2011, pp. 86–104.

Weatherston, Rosemary. "An Interview with Cherríe Moraga." *Queer Frontiers: Millennial Geographies, Genders, and Generations*, edited by Joseph A. Boone et al., U of Wisconsin P, 2000, pp. 64–83.

Williams, Emma. "Who *Really* Needs a 'Theory' of Mind?" *Against Theory of Mind*, edited by Ivan Leudar and Alan Costall, Palgrave Macmillan, 2009, pp. 144–66.

Wimmer, Heinz, et al. "A Second Stage in Children's Conception of Mental Life: Understanding Informational Accesses as Origins of Knowledge and Belief." *Developing Theories of Mind,* edited by Janet W. Astington et al., Cambridge UP, 1988, pp. 173–92.

Wispé, Lauren. *The Psychology of Sympathy.* Plenum, 1991.

Yasmin. Comment on *Butterfly Boy.* Goodreads.com, 22 Jan. 2012, www.goodreads.com/review/show/266210694.

Zunshine, Lisa. "Theory of Mind and Fictions of Embodied Transparency." *Theory of Mind in Literature,* edited by Paula Leverage et al., Purdue UP, 2011, pp. 63–91.

———. "Theory of Mind and Michael Fried's *Absorption Theatricality*: Notes toward Cognitive Historicism." *Toward a Cognitive Theory of Narrative Acts,* edited by Frederick Luis Aldama, U of Texas P, 2010, pp. 179–203.

———. *Why We Read Fiction.* Ohio State UP, 2006.

INDEX

academia: and Chicana feminism, 126n7; and close reading, 16–17; on commodification of literature, 115–16; and gay Chicano literature/studies, 4, 6n6; use of genre in, 5
activism, 157
affect in works of Rigoberto González, 22–23, 35, 46, 49. *See also* affective plane
affective plane, 17, 32; in *Butterfly Boy* (González), 46, 52, 55; in *Crossing Vines* (González), 23, 33, 34, 36; function of, 23
Alarcón, Francisco X., 2, 2n1, 15, 139, 159, 163
Aldama, Frederick Luis, 86n1, 100, 116, 122, 122n3, 123, 128, 138, 160n1
Algonquin Press, 12, 85, 120, 148, 150
Allende, Isabel, 87, 99
Almaguer, Tomás, 4
altruism, 24, 44, 133, 133n10, 134
Alvarez, Julia, 90n4, 123
Alvarez, Pablo, 1, 137

Amazon.com, 122, 123n4, 139–41, 140n13, 140n14
ambassadorship, cultural, 126
Anaya, Rudolfo, 91, 100, 124, 145
Anderson, Chris, 140, 140n13
Anzaldúa, Gloria, 3n3, 126n7, 141
Arguedas, José María, 125–26, 127n7
Association of Jotería Arts, Activism, and Scholarship, 5
audience: implied, 29; overheard, 135–37; represented, 29; reviews and reception of works, 21–22, 112, 121–22, 136; sympathetic, 137–38. *See also* reader
author: implied, 38, 76n10; real, 38, 39n11; represented, 38, 39n11, 41, 46. *See also* individual author names
awards, 6n6, 151–53, 162–63

Bal, Mieke, 59
Bañalez, Xamuel, 3n3
Baron-Cohen, Simon, 62n3
Batson, Daniel C., 29

178 • INDEX

Bauman, Zygmunt, 91–92, 100, 116, 132
belief change, 95, 102, 107–8
best-sellers, list of, 122–23
bildungsroman, 46
blanks, narrative. *See* gaps
blurbs. *See* reviews
bookstore, 116, 119n2
Booth, Wayne C., 58–59, 76n10
Bourtolussi, Marisa. *See* *Psychonarratology*
branding: of gay Chicano authors, 127–28; of Latinx literature, 86, 89, 91, 117, 119; and magical realism, 86, 91. *See also* commodification; market, literary
Brewer, William F., 96
Bruce-Novoa, Juan, 4, 160
Butterfly Boy (González), 45–46, 78, 109; analysis of, 48–55; cultural schema in, 55; empathy in, 50, 52, 131n9; intended readership of, 135; reader reviews of, 136; and reader solidarity, 131n9; use of language in, 117n1

capitalism, 91–92, 122n3
Carroll, Noel, 25, 131
Carruthers, Peter, 62n3
Castelfranchi, Cristiano, 95, 100, 102, 107
Castillo, Ana, 119, 126n7
catharsis, 55
Catholic, 83
Central Valley (California), 78–79, 153–54
Chaminade, Thierry, 28
characters: animation of, 63n5, 64; infantilization of, 44–45, 56; language use of, 117n1; reader identification with, 22, 27n4, 47–48, 130–31; reader solidarity with, 131, 131n9, 132
Chatman, Seymour, 31, 38, 59, 76n10

Chevalier, Judith A., 140
Chicana feminists, 2, 3n4, 155; relationship with Euro-American feminists, 126n7, 151; relationship with gay Latinx men, 3n4
childhood, 16, 49–50, 53–54
Cisneros, Sandra, 121, 123, 124n5, 125, 145
Clark, Candice, 35, 136. *See also* credits, sympathy
class, social, 41, 44, 117n1, 129, 159
classroom, 141; narrative analysis in, 38; place of gay Chicano literature in, 5; reader response in, 21–22, 41
close reading, 16; criticism of, 12; utility of, 13
closet, the, 3n4, 50, 137, 156, 163
closure, narrative: law of (Tan), 45; narrator and, 61, 65–67; search for in works of Muñoz, 58, 68–72, 74
cognition. *See* empathy; genric schema; product design; schema; surprise; sympathy; theory of mind
cognitive slippage, 63–64, 130
coming-out story, 9, 11, 50, 152
commodification: benefits of, 123–24, 128; of gay Chicano literature, 19; and genre, 116; and homogenization, 124; of Latinx literature, 119, 122; as literary theme, 144; and publishers, 18
community: Chicanx, 78, 153–55; importance of in Latinx literature, 109–10; LGBT, 133; queer white, 77n11, 151–52. *See also* branding; market, literary
consumer, 116–17, 119, 139–40, 140n14. *See also* reader
Cornejo Polar, Antonio, 125
Corral, Eduardo C., 162

Cosmides, Leda, 45
Cotera, Marta, 126n7
cover, book, 44, 78, 86, 119–21, 127
crack manifesto, 87, 87n2
credits, sympathy, 35–36, 136
Crossing Vines (González), 56, 78, 109; affective plane in, 33, 55; analysis of, 33–37, 39–45, book cover of, 120; intended readership of, 135; narrator, 30–31, 39–40; plot summary, 30; and reader politics, 131–33; student response to, 21–22, 44; sympathy in, 33, 41, 130–31; use of language in, 117n1
Cuadros, Gil, 1, 138, 159
cultural narrative (Phelan), 8–9
cultural schema, 17–18: criticism of, 17; definition of, 9, 9n7; and expectations of literature. 44, 51, 54; and genric schema, 11; and intended reader, 137–38; potential exclusivity of, 71; and unintended reader, 135; in works of Espinoza, 88, 111; in works of González, 23, 41, 43, 48, 51, 54–55; in works of Muñoz, 58, 65, 67, 71, 77–78, 83

Danielson, Marivel T., 14
Decety, Jean, 28
Díaz, Junot, 122, 126, 145
diversity, 111
Dixon, Peter. See *Psychonarratology*

Eggum, Natalie, 25, 130
Eisenburg, Nancy, 25, 130
emotion: A/R (Tan), 22, 45; negative, 25n3, 133; universal, 27n4. See also empathy; sympathy
emotional memory, 26
empathy, 23; ambassadorial strategic (Keen) 47, 54–55; bounded strategic (Keen) 47, 50, 54; broadcast strategic (Keen) 48; cross empathy, 54; definition of, 24, 26–28; and democracy, 133; as distinct from sympathy, 25, 28–29; and justice, 132–33; and reader politics, 129, 130–33, 136–38. See also *Butterfly Boy*
Espinoza, Alex, 89, 121; comparisons to other authors, 145; interview with, 144–47, 150–52, 155–56; origin of writing, 144; publishing outcomes, 85
Esquivel, Laura, 87, 90, 144
ethnography, literature as, 86n1, 124–25

Faith Healer of Olive Avenue, The (Muñoz), 57, 60, 75n9, 77–78; book cover of, 120, branding as gay literature, 127; stories:
"Brother John," 83
"The Heart Finds its own Conclusion," 74–75
"Lindo y Querido," 60, 148
"When You Come into Your Kingdom," 66
fellow feeling, 24
Fish, Stanley, 135
Five Acts of Diego León, The (Espinoza), 78, 110n16; branding as gay literature, 127; intended readership of, 135; origin of, 146–47; political function of, 133; publishing of, 147; and reader politics, 130–32; reader reviews of, 136–37; reviews of, 150–52
flash fiction, 73
Fludernick, Monika, 73
fMRI, 27, 27n3, 92n6
focalization, 31–32, 70, 80; and narrator role, 31. See also spatiotemporal shift
Foster, David William, 4, 14, 160

Gallese, Vittorio, 2
Galloway-Thomas, Carolyn, 132
gaps, narrative: definition of, 65–67; reader filling of, 100; in works of Manuel Muñoz, 60, 65–67, 69–73, 73n8, 74–75, 76n10, 148
García Landa, José Ángel, 135
García Márquez, Gabriel, 87, 121, 145
gay Chicano literature and authors: academic study of, 6n6, 160; branding as gay, 127; community of, 155; future of, 156–57; as genre, 4–5, 115–16, 139–41, 160–63; history/timeline of, 2, 2n1, 6n6, 11, 139, 159; literary themes of, 78, 159; poetry, 162; and publishing, 12, 85; use in the classroom, 5. *See also* individual author names
Gay Latino Studies (Hames-Garcia and Martínez), 5
gay marriage, 133, 134
gender roles, 50–51, 53
Genette, Gérard, 30, 58
genre, 10; building of, 4–5, 14, 115–16, 139–41, 160–61, 162–63; commodifying impulse of, 116; formation, role of internet in, 139; importance of, 1; and readers, 4. *See also* genric schema; gay Chicano literature and authors: as genre
genric schema: and branding, 117; and cultural schema, 11; definition of, 10; of Latinx literature, 11, 88, 102; of magical realism, 86 (*see also* magical realism); and readers, 11, 88; and reader expectation of literature, 99, 108
Goldie, Peter, 26
Gomez, Marga, 16, 17
González, Rigoberto: academic study of, 6n6; access to publishers, 153; branding as gay author, 127; interviews of, 18, 152–53, 155–57; origin of writing, 149–50; publishing outcomes, 85; relationship with literary community, 152–53, 155; reviews of works, 122. *See also Butterfly Boy*; *Crossing Vines*
goodreads.com, 112, 136–37, 140–41

Hames-Garcia, Michael, 3n3, 5
Hernández, Ellie, 12
heterogeneity, 125
heteronormative, 126, 128
HIV/AIDS, 2n1, 3, 159
Hoeken, Hans, 97
Hoffman, Martin L., 130, 133
Hogan, Patrick Colm, 8, 26, 117
homogenization of literature, 124, 126
homophobia, 50, 52, 55, 159
homosexuality as hidden and shameful, 58, 70–72, 73n8, 75, 78, 83

identification, reader with literature, 1, 8, 130–31
implied author, 38, 76n10
implied reader, 37–39, 47, 134
injustice, 132–33
interest, reader, 58
internet, role in genre formation, 139
Iran-Nejad, Asghar, 92n6, 97
Iser, Wolfgang, 39, 65, 73, 134
Islas, Arturo, 2, 78, 128, 159

jacket, book, 44, 78, 86, 119–21, 127
Jotería studies and scholarship, 3n3, 5, 15–16, 160; and literary analysis, 6. *See also* queer Latinx studies
joto, discussion of term, 3n3
judgment, 32, 80, 81
justice, 132–33

Kagan, Jerome, 99n11
Kanellos, Nicolás, 109
Keen, Suzanne: *Empathy and the Novel*, 46; "Narrative Empathy," 24, 27n4, 29, 47–48, 54–55, 130; *Narrative Form*, 40, 141. *See also* empathy
Kim, Sue J., 44–45, 125, 130
kinship, 112, 131
Kintsch, Walter, 96, 99
Kreuzbauer, Robert, 117, 121
Kuiken, Don, 32

La Fountain-Stokes, Lawrence, 77, 77n11
labor exploitation, 41–43
Lambda Literary, 151
Lamm, Claus, 28
language, use of in Chicanx literature, 117n1
Latin American literature and authors, 89n3; connection to Latinx literature, 89; and magical realism, 86–87. *See also individual author names*
Latinx literature and authors: access to publishers, 117n.1, 122, 153; branding of, 91, 109, 119; as foreign, 89, 120; homogenization of, 124, 126; language use in, 117n1; and magical realism, 109; market link to Latin American literature, 89; as niche, 122, 128; and reader response, 126; relation to wider queer literary community, 151–53; sales of, 123–24; literary themes of, 109, 147. *See also individual author names*
Law & Order, 100–101, 107
Leverage, Paula, 62n3
Lichtenstein, Edward H., 96
Life in Search of Readers (Martín-Rodríguez): branding of Latinx literature, 10, 119; commodification of Latinx literature, 116; discussion of book reviews, 121; language in Latinx literature, 117n1; Latinx literature and magical realism, 86, 88–89; transculturation, 124–25
long tail, 123; and Amazon.com, 140, 140n13
Lorini, Emiliano, 95, 100, 102, 107

magical realism, 10, 18, 86, 86n1, 88; and branding, 90–91, 99; and Latin American literature, 87; and Latinx community, 145; and Latinx literature, 109; and reader expectation, 99n11, 106, 108; and reviews, 121; in *Still Water Saints* (Espinoza), 144–45; and surprise, 99
magical realization, 88, 108; definition/process of, 87; of Latinx literature, 89–90
Malter, Alan J., 117, 121
Manrique, Jaime, 3n3
maricón, 3n3, 50
mariposa, definition of, 3n3
market, literary, 86–87, 89, 89n3, 138, 140n13; as heteronormative, 126–28; of Latinx literature, 90n4, 117n1, 122, 122n3, 126–28; and marketa, 117n1; use of data from, 141. *See also* branding, commodification
Márquez, Gabriel García. *See* García Márquez, Gabriel
Marshall, David, 24
Martín-Rodríguez, Manuel-M. *See Life in Search of Readers*
Martínez, Ernesto, 3n3, 6, 15, 70, 70n7, 143
masculinity, 155, 159
materialism, 109n15

Matravers, Derek, 26
Mayzlin, Dina, 140
McCracken, Ellen, 90n4, 124n5
mentorship, 156
Meyer, Wulf-Uwe, 92–93
Miall, David S., 32
Michalska, Kalina J., 28
Michelon, Pascale, 92n6
Miller, David, 133n10
mind reading. *See* theory of mind
Mitchell, Peter, 61
Moraga, Cherríe, 3n4, 126n7, 160
morality, 129, 131, 133
Morrell, Michael E., 133
Moya, Paula, 6n6, 7–8, 12–13, 70–71, 132, 143
Muñoz, José Esteban, 16–17
Muñoz, Manuel, 57, 82–83; intended readership of, 135; interview with, 70, 147–48, 150, 151–57; on publishing, 16, 82n13; publishing outcomes, 85, 148–49; reviews of works, 122; use of trauma, 148, 162; on use of word queer, 3n3, 152; writing style of, 143, 148. *See also individual works*
Murphy, Miguel, 162
mysticism, 86, 91, 102, 104, 106, 108, 121–22

narratee, 38, 40
narration shift, 23
narrative: cultural, 8–9; embedded, 64; push-pull, in works of Muñoz, 58, 65, 67, 70, 72, 74–75, 81–82; rug-pull, 98, 101. *See also* gaps; closure
narrator: autodiegetic, 48; confrontational/judgmental, 78, 80–81; continuing consciousness of, 65; emotive, 79; extradiegetic, 31; first-person, 32; as focalizer, 31; integrity of, 76n10; motivations of, 58, 61; omniscient, 79, reader perception of, 38, 39n11, 59; second-person, 57, 73; as story guide, 60, 66; studies of, 58–60; third-person, 32, 57, 60; unreliable, 39n11, 59, 76, 76n10; vague, 18, 58, 67, 70, 73, 75, 76n10, 83; we, 80–81; in works of Manuel Muñoz generally, 57

Nava, Michael, 2, 2n1, 127–28, 159
Niepal, Michael, 92
Nishida, Hiroko, 9n7
Northwestern University Press, 85, 148
Nünning, Ansgar, 76n10

Oatley, Keith, 64
Ortony, Andrew, 92n5, 94

Palmer, Alan, 64
Paredes, Raymund A., 128
Partridge, Derek, 92n5, 94
Pérez, Daniel Enrique, 3n3, 6n6
Pérez, Hiram, 14
perspective: external, 32; internal, 31–32; minority, 15; narrator, 38, 76n10; shifting, 26. *See also* focalization
Phelan, Jim, 8, 31, 76n10, 77; cultural narrative, 8–9; layered ethical situation, 77; theory of narrative, 32, 39, 45, 51
poetry, 162
postdictability, 96, 98, 107, 113. *See also* predictability; surprise
poststructuralism, 6, 12
predictability, 100–101, 113. *See also* postdictability; surprise
Premack, David, 62n3
Prince, Gerald, 31, 59

proattitude, 25, 130. *See also* prosocial behavior
product design, 117
prosocial behavior, 25, 130, 133. *See also* proattitude
Psycho, 101n12, 153
Psychonarratology (Bourtolussi and Dixon), 32, 38, 39n11, 59, 64–65
publishing and publishers, 90; as gatekeepers, 115; and gay Chicano authors, 85; treatment of Latinx authors, 122, 122n3. *See also* Random House; Algonquin Press; Northwestern University Press

queer: and whiteness, 3n3, 153; term in comparison to joto, 3n3
Queer in Aztlán (Del Castillo and Güido), 1, 3–5, 160, 163
queer Latinx studies, 13. *See also* Jotería studies
queer representation: audience interpretation of, 15; critical interpretation of, 16; externalization/internalization of, 16–17; first discovery of, 7–8; power of, 13–15

racism, 34, 79n12, 126n7, 159
Rama, Ángel, 125
Random House, 12, 85, 88, 90, 117n1, 137, 147
Ratcliffe, Sophie, 24
reader: arousal in text, 58; identification with text, 1, 8, 130–31; imperfect, 39; implied, 37–39, 47, 134; informed, 135; intended, 47, 53–55, 135–36; potential, 86, 90, 102, 116–17, 121; real, 38; reasons for liking of text, 97, 138; represented, 29, 39, 39n11, 40–41, 44, 46–47, 135; unintended, 135–37; and use of politics in text, 129–38
reader expectation of literature, 44, 55, 100; and magical realism, 99, 99n11, 100; and schema, 44, 51, 99, 132; and *Still Water Saints*, 86, 90–91, 102, 106, 145; and surprise, 101. *See also* audience
reader response theory, 21, 22n1
realist position, 15–16
Rechy, John, 1–2, 2n1, 123, 127–28, 159
Red-Inked Retablos (González), 2, 4, 6, 19, 163
Reisenzein, Rainer, 93–94
reviews, 86; back of book, 121–22; consumer consideration of, 140n14; difficulties in author access to, 150–53
Rice-González, Charles, 139
Richards, Ivor Armstrong, 22n1
Rivera, Tomas, 150
Robbins, Jill, 89n3
Roberts, Nancy, 23
Rodríguez, Juana, 13n9
Rodriguez, Richard, 2, 159
Rodríguez, Richard T., 2n2, 112
rug-pull, narrative, 98, 101
Rulfo, Juan, 87

Sáenz, Benjamin Alire, 2, 6n6, 141, 162
sales, book, 89, 119n2, 122–24, 140–41, 140n13; use of in studies, 141
Sánchez, Alex, 2, 6n6, 163
Scheff, Thomas J., 55
schema: and cultural identification, 9; definition of, 8, 93; history of theory, 9n7, of Latinx literature, 119; of readers, 132; of story structure, 96–97; and surprise, 101–2, 107–8; vestigial (Moya), 71. *See also* genric schema

Schützwohl, Achim, 93
Schwatrz, Barry, 116
Seglow, Jonathan, 133n10
self-identification, 3n3, 152
shame of homosexuality, 58, 70–72, 73n8, 75, 77n11, 78, 83
Shott, Susan, 133
simulation theory, 26
Singer, Tania, 28, 130
slippage, cognitive, 64
solidarity with characters, 131, 131n9, 132
Soto, Sandra K., 13
spatiotemporal shift, 32; in *Crossing Vines* (González), 33–34, 36–37
Spolsky, Ellen, 65
Stanzel, F. K., 60
Steuber, Karsten R., 26
Still Water Saints, 60, 88; analysis of, 103–7, 110–12; and belief change, 108; book cover of, 120–21; in bookstores, 119n2; branding of, 86, 91, 99; and magical realism, 144–45; reader expectation of, 86, 90–91, 102, 106, 108; reader reviews of, 112; reviews of, 121–22; structure of, 90; use of language in, 117n1
structuralism, 12
surprise: and artificial intelligence, 92n5; as astonishment, 101, 101n12, 102n13; and belief change, 107; as expectation failure, 94–95; expected and unexpected, 101, 103; literary research of, 96–98; in literature, 92; and magical realism, 99; and postdictability, 96, 98; and reader appreciation of literature, 97; as schema mismatch, 101; scientific research of, 93–95; in *Still Water Saints*, 88

sympathy: credits, 35–36, 136; in *Crossing Vines*, 33–35, 41–45; definition of, 24–25; as distinct from empathy, 25, 28–29; as inclusive of empathy, 24, 27n4; and justness, 35; and race, 79n12; and reader politics, 129–32, 136–38; and schema change, 102; and selfish vindication, 24, 131; in works of Muñoz, 79–80. *See also* empathy

Tan, Ed S., 22, 45, 58, 132
theory of mind: criticism of, 64n6; definition of, 61–62; history of, 62n3; and human development, 62n3; and narrators, 58, 61; and readers, 98; in study of literature, 63
Tobin, Vera, 97–98, 101n12
Tongson, Karen, 111
Tooby, John, 25
Torres, Hector A., 128
Torres, Justin, 141
transculturation, 124, 125
transgender, 156
trauma, 148, 162
tropicalization, 89
Trout, J. D., 129, 131

understanding, cross, 54–55
undocumented, 137, 156
United Farm Works Union, 42
unreliable narrator, 39n11, 59, 76, 76n10
Urroz, Eloy, 87

Van Lange, Paul A. M., 133
Van Peer, Willie, 35
Vargas Llosa, Mario, 87
Vermuele, Blakey, 41, 63n5
VIDA count, 150
Vignemont, Frédérique de, 27

Viramontes, Helena Maria, 157
Von Vliet, Mario, 97

we groups, 131
What You See in the Dark (Muñoz), 57, 66, 82, 109, 128; book cover of, 120; lack of reviews of, 150–51; origin of, 153–54; response from Latinx literary community, 154; student response to, 21–22
Will & Grace, 134
Wimmer, Heinz, 62n3
Wispé, Lauren, 24, 25n3, 131
Woodruff, Guy, 62n3

Zigzagger, 57, 75n9, 77–78, 82; arrangement of stories, 78, 148; book cover of, 120, 127, branding as gay literature, 127; and the coming-out story, 152; origin of, 152; publishing of, 147–48; and reader sympathy, 130–31; stories:
"By the Time You Get There, by the Time You Get Back," 77
"Campo," 76n10
"Good as Yesterday," 77–78
"Monkey Sí," 78–82, 131, 137, 149, 159
"Skyshot," 77
"Swallow," 73–74
"Tiburón," 77
"The Unimportant Lila Parr," 71–72, 137, 148
"Zigzagger," 67–72, 74
Zunshine, Lisa, 61, 63, 63n4, 130

COGNITIVE APPROACHES TO CULTURE
FREDERICK LUIS ALDAMA, PATRICK COLM HOGAN,
LALITA PANDIT HOGAN, AND SUE J. KIM, SERIES EDITORS

This series takes up cutting edge research in a broad range of cognitive sciences insofar as this research bears on and illuminates cultural phenomena such as literature, film, drama, music, dance, visual art, digital media, and comics, among others. For the purpose of the series, "cognitive science" is construed broadly to encompass work derived from cognitive and social psychology, neuroscience, cognitive and generative linguistics, affective science, and related areas in anthropology, philosophy, computer science, and elsewhere. Though open to all forms of cognitive analysis, the series is particularly interested in works that explore the social and political consequences of cognitive cultural study.

Capturing Mariposas: Reading Cultural Schema in Gay Chicano Literature
  DOUG P. BUSH

Necessary Nonsense: Aesthetics, History, Neurology, Psychology
  IRVING MASSEY

Shaming into Brown: Somatic Transactions of Race in Latina/o Literature
  STEPHANIE FETTA

Resilient Memories: Amerindian Cognitive Schemas in Latin American Art
  ARIJ OUWENEEL

Permissible Narratives: The Promise of Latino/a Literature
  CHRISTOPHER GONZÁLEZ

Literatures of Liberation: Non-European Universalisms and Democratic Progress
  MUKTI LAKHI MANGHARAM

Affective Ecologies: Empathy, Emotion, and Environmental Narrative
  ALEXA WEIK VON MOSSNER

A Passion for Specificity: Confronting Inner Experience in Literature and Science
  MARCO CARACCIOLO AND RUSSELL T. HURLBURT